I0887287

City Blocks

Denise Russell

LEISURE ARTS, INC. • Maumelle, Arkansas

I AM A CITY GIRL.

Born in São Paulo, Brazil, I have lived in or close to large cities most of my life. Fast forward a few decades and you will find me living in the US, raising three boys alongside my soul mate, and designing and making quilts. I am blessed beyond measure to be doing something I am passionate about! I love creating projects with fabrics of every color, piecing quilts, appliquéing whimsical blocks, and adding embroidery accents to my work. When I work with colorful fabrics, whether in my studio or with the computer as I design quilt projects for fabric makers, my mind goes to faraway places: grapes and purples transport me to Italy with its vast vineyards, blue and turquoise send me to the ocean, and vibrant hues take me back to Carnival – the annual Mardi Gras celebration in Brazil. Mine is a fantastic pursuit!

A little while ago I decided to celebrate my love for city living by designing a quilt which would depict activities, places and landmarks one would likely find in any city. The City Blocks quilt began as a Sew Along on my blog, Pieced Brain, when every two weeks I would release a new block. Combining quilters' perennial passions - piecing and appliqué – I designed unique blocks with simple lines and construction, suitable for beginners yet interesting for seasoned quilters. It also included a block with a city directory much like the ones you find downtown.

The City Blocks quilt I share with you here is identical to the first one I made with the same whimsical look. It measures $68^1/_4$" x $88^1/_2$" with 8" blocks. The blocks are divided into thirty-one colorful and bright pieced or appliquéd blocks portraying common city sights and places such as parks, libraries, restaurants, ice cream shops, gym, pool, etc. They are modern and full of movement, alternating with simple chain blocks representing the 'grid' or intersections of a busy city. The directory block has a map as its backdrop. As laid out, the quilt groups the blocks into a business district, residential and commercial areas, entertainment venues, a harbor, and modes of transportation.

The City Blocks quilt is an ideal project for pre-cuts or as a stash buster. Audition all the pieces of fabrics and label them with the name of the block in which they will shine. As you do so, think of companion projects such as pillows, wall hangings, table runners, and totes showcasing your most frequented places or blocks with a special meaning to you or to the gift recipient. Choose fabrics from various collections: each business location in a city has its own personality and your fabric selection can reflect it. I designed my City Blocks quilt with fabrics by Blank Quilting and Studioe who graciously provided their beautiful prints and solids for this project.

You can make it to celebrate your love for city living as I did, or you may want to create your own city by customizing the directory block with the names of your favorite ice cream shop, park, coffee shop, or restaurant. The quilt can also be a memory quilt where you record where you raised your family or an imaginary city with sites from all your trips.

Do you have a college-bound child, or a married child or friend who is moving to a new city? The City Blocks quilt would be the perfect gift to remind them of the moments you shared, or to encourage them to create memories in their new surroundings. How about making it as a wedding anniversary quilt for your parents as a creative snapshot of weekly family trips to town for grocery shopping, watching a movie, or borrowing books from the library? After all, memories are made every day, not just during those once-a-year vacations…

Whether you are a city girl like me, or just fall in love with this quilt, I hope the next pages will inspire you to become the master planner of a community all your own. Share your project on social media using the hash tag **#citygirlquilt** for all of us to enjoy your interpretation of the City Blocks quilt.

DENISE RUSSELL

CONTENTS

DEDICATION

To my mother Eunice - the ultimate city girl - whose creativity, resourcefulness, and fearless attitude never cease to amaze and inspire me.

CITY BLOCKS QUILT

Finished Quilt Size: $68^{1}/_{4}$" x $88^{1}/_{2}$" (173 cm x 225 cm)
Finished Block Size: 8" x 8" (20 cm x 20 cm)

SHOPPING LIST

Yardage is based on 43"/44" (109 cm/112 cm) wide fabric with a usable width of 40" (102 cm). This quilt is perfect for fabric scraps left over from other projects. However, if you choose to buy fabrics or feel that you don't have enough fabric in your stash, here's the approximate total yardage you will need to complete the quilt. I've broken the yardage down into color families. Refer to the ***Featured Blocks****, pages 6-66, for specific fabric requirements.*

For Featured Blocks:

- ☐ $^{1}/_{2}$ yd (46 cm) **total** of assorted blue print fabrics
- ☐ $^{3}/_{8}$ yd (34 cm) **total** of assorted red print fabrics
- ☐ $^{1}/_{2}$ yd (46 cm) **total** of assorted green print fabrics
- ☐ $^{3}/_{8}$ yd (34 cm) **total** of assorted yellow print fabrics
- ☐ $^{1}/_{4}$ yd (23 cm) **total** of assorted orange print fabrics
- ☐ $^{3}/_{8}$ yd (34 cm) **total** of assorted pink print fabrics
- ☐ $^{1}/_{4}$ yd (23 cm) **total** of assorted purple print fabrics
- ☐ $^{1}/_{2}$ yd (46 cm) **total** of assorted teal/aqua print fabrics
- ☐ $^{5}/_{8}$ yd (57 cm) **total** of assorted white print fabrics
- ☐ $^{3}/_{8}$ yd (34 cm) **total** of assorted cream/beige print fabrics
- ☐ $^{5}/_{8}$ yd (57 cm) **total** of assorted gray print fabrics
- ☐ $^{3}/_{4}$ yd (69 cm) **total** of assorted black print fabrics

For Alternate Blocks, Sashings, and Cornerstones:

- ☐ $1^{1}/_{8}$ yds (1 m) of white solid fabric for alternate blocks
- ☐ $1^{7}/_{8}$ yds (1.7 m) of light gray/ white dot print fabric for sashings
- ☐ $1^{1}/_{4}$ yds (1.1 m) of medium gray dot print fabric for alternate blocks and cornerstones
- ☐ $1^{1}/_{4}$ yds (1.1 m) of dark gray solid fabric for alternate blocks and cornerstones

For Finishing:

- ☐ 76" x 97" (193 cm x 246 cm) piece of batting
- ☐ $5^{5}/_{8}$ yds (5.1 m) of fabric for backing and hanging sleeve
- ☐ $^{3}/_{4}$ yd (69 m) of fabric for binding

You will also need:

- ☐ paper-backed fusible web
- ☐ coordinating thread for piecing
- ☐ matching threads for machine appliqué
- ☐ fabric marker
- ☐ 1 sheet of printable fabric
- ☐ ink jet printer
- ☐ Microsoft Word template

CUTTING THE ALTERNATE BLOCKS, SASHINGS, AND CORNERSTONES

Follow ***Rotary Cutting****, page 86, to cut fabric. Cut all strips from the selvage-to-selvage width of the fabric. All measurements include $^{1}/_{4}$" seam allowances.*

From white solid fabric:

- Cut 4 strips $4^{1}/_{2}$" x fabric width.
- Cut 4 strips $4^{1}/_{2}$" x fabric width. From these strips, cut 64 rectangles $2^{1}/_{2}$" x $4^{1}/_{2}$".

From light gray/white dot print fabric:

- Cut 7 strips $8^{1}/_{2}$" x fabric width. From these strips, cut 110 sashings $2^{1}/_{2}$" x $8^{1}/_{2}$".

From medium gray dot print fabric:

- Cut 8 strips $4^{1}/_{2}$" x fabric width.
- Cut 2 strips $2^{1}/_{2}$" x fabric width. From these strips, cut 24 squares $2^{1}/_{2}$" x $2^{1}/_{2}$".

From dark gray solid fabric:

- Cut 8 strips $4^{1}/_{2}$" x fabric width.
- Cut 2 strips $2^{1}/_{2}$" x fabric width. From these strips, cut 24 squares $2^{1}/_{2}$" x $2^{1}/_{2}$".

From fabric for binding:

- Cut 9 **binding strips** $2^{1}/_{2}$" wide.

Quilted by Melissa Kelly from Sew Shabby Quilting

FEATURED BLOCKS

COURTHOUSE

WHAT YOU'LL NEED

- ☐ 1 yellow print rectangle for background 10" x 16", cut into:
  - 2 strips (A) 1" x 4$^1/_2$".
  - 4 squares (B) 1$^1/_2$" x 1$^1/_2$".
  - 1 strip (C) 1$^1/_2$" x 7".
  - 1 strip (D) 1$^1/_2$" x 8$^1/_2$".
  - 2 rectangles (E) 2$^1/_2$" x 4$^1/_2$".
- ☐ 1 gray print rectangle for columns 8" x 16", cut into:
  - 6 strips (F) 1$^1/_2$" x 2$^1/_2$".
  - 3 strips (G) 1$^1/_2$" x 4$^1/_2$".
  - 1 strip (H) 1$^1/_2$" x 7".

BLOCK

TIP

To prevent the corners of small pieces of fabric from being stuck under the sewing machine plate, or thread from pooling under the fabric, begin sewing onto a double fabric scrap then sew straight onto your block. The sewing area stays neater also, as beginning threads (and ending ones if you choose to sew another scrap at the end of the seam) are contained. As a bonus, your clothes won't look like fiber art.

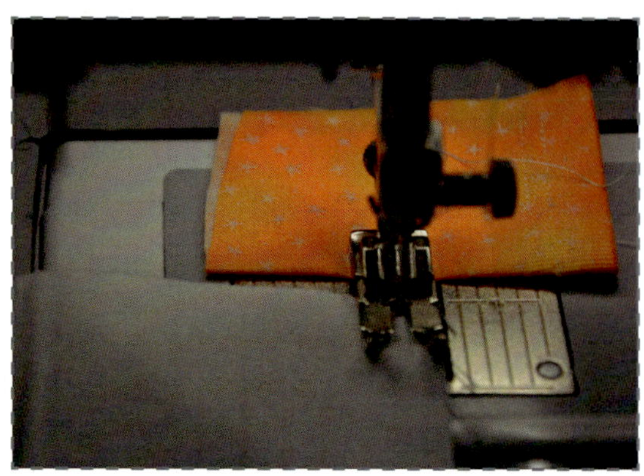

ASSEMBLY

*Follow **Machine Piecing**, page 86, and **Pressing**, page 87, to make block. Use a ¼" seam allowance throughout.*

1. Sew strips C and H together. Do not press open. Cut this strip set into four 1½" sections. Press the sections open and sew them together to make **Unit 1**.
2. Alternately sew three F strips and two B squares together to make **Unit 2**. Repeat to make two strips.
3. Make the block center by sewing in this order: one A strip, one G strip, one E rectangle, one G strip, one E rectangle, one G strip, and one A strip **(Unit 3)**.
4. Arrange and sew the block together in rows to make the **Block**: The D strip, Unit 1, Unit 2, Unit 3, and the other Unit 2.

Unit 1

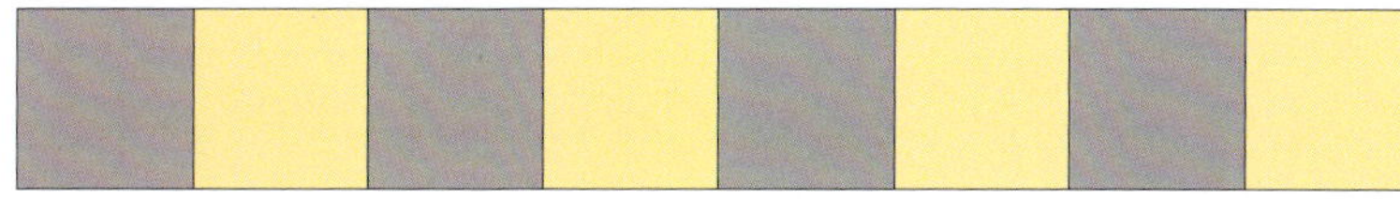

Unit 2 (make 2)

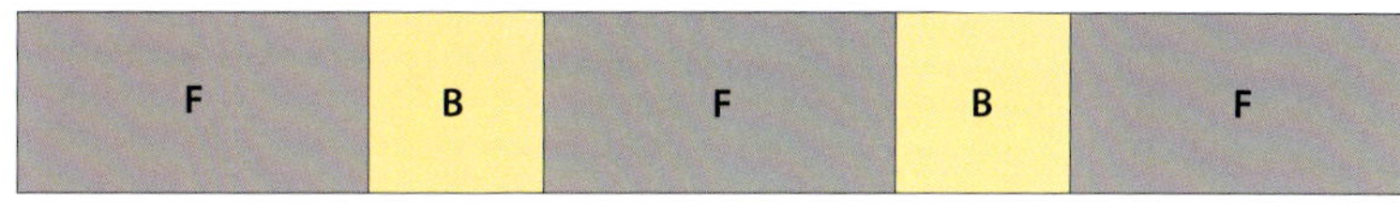

Unit 3

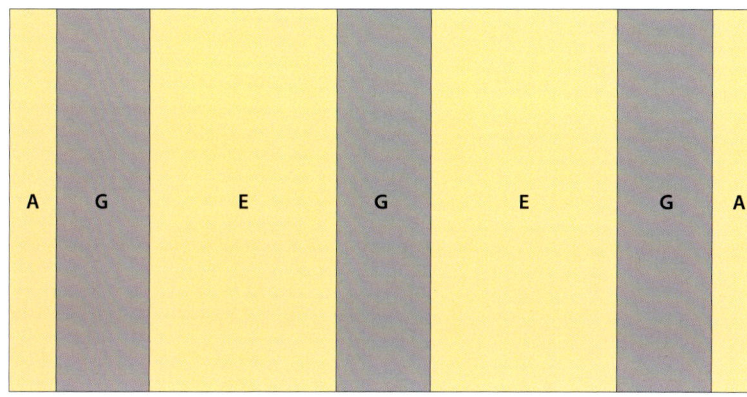

COURTHOUSE

The Courthouse in São Paulo, Brazil, is a magnificent building with marble and granite. Its columns are reminiscent of the Courthouse in Rome and became the focal point of my block.

THE HOTEL

WHAT YOU'LL NEED

- ☐ 1 marbled pink print background square 9" x 9"
- ☐ 1 purple print rectangle for the roof $2^1/_2$" x 10"
- ☐ 1 black/white check rectangle for sheet and pillowcase $4^1/_2$" x $5^1/_2$"
- ☐ 1 black tone-on-tone print strip for bed posts $1^1/_2$" x 9"

ASSEMBLY

1. Follow **Preparing Fusible Appliqués**, page 88, and use patterns to cut appliqués.
2. Position the appliqués on the background square and fuse them according to the fusible web manufacturer's instructions.
3. Follow **Blanket Stitch Appliqué**, page 88, to appliqué pieces in place using matching thread.
4. Trim block to $8^1/_2$" x $8^1/_2$".

BLOCK

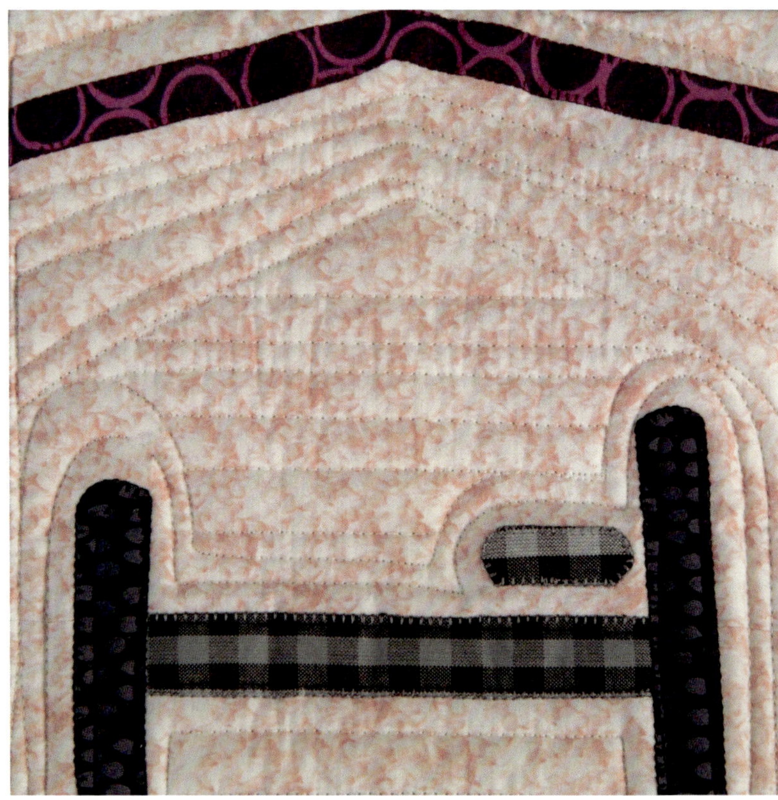

TIP:
To remove the fusible web backing easily, run the tip of a pin over the backing paper without going through the fabric to rip it. Then, pull paper away from the fabric.

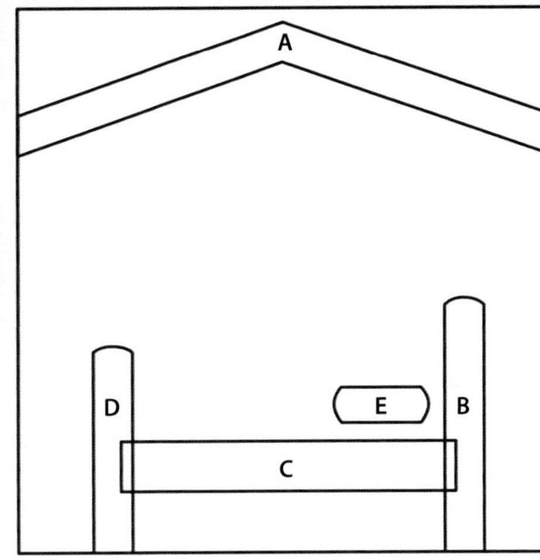
A
D
E
B
C

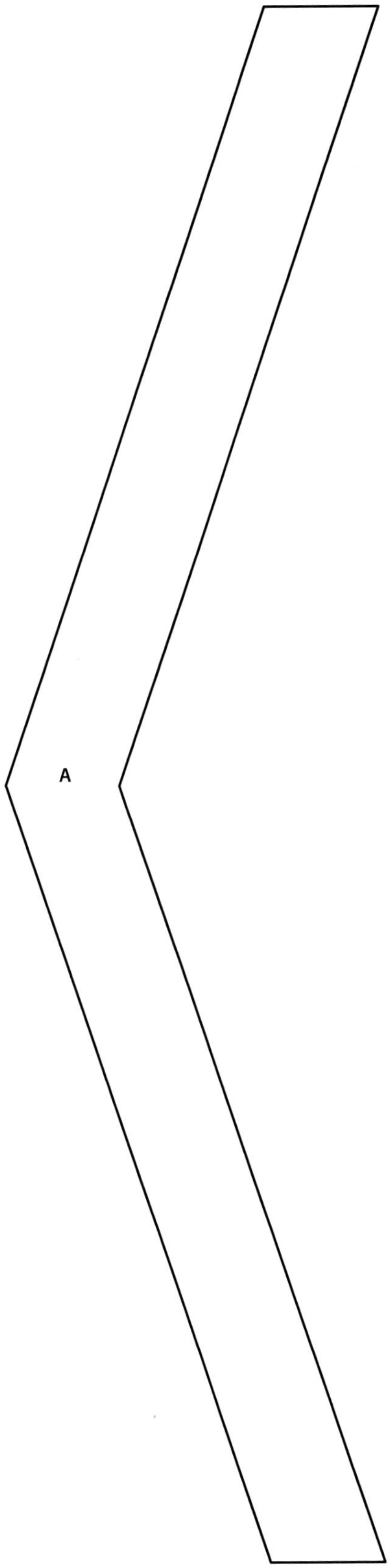
A

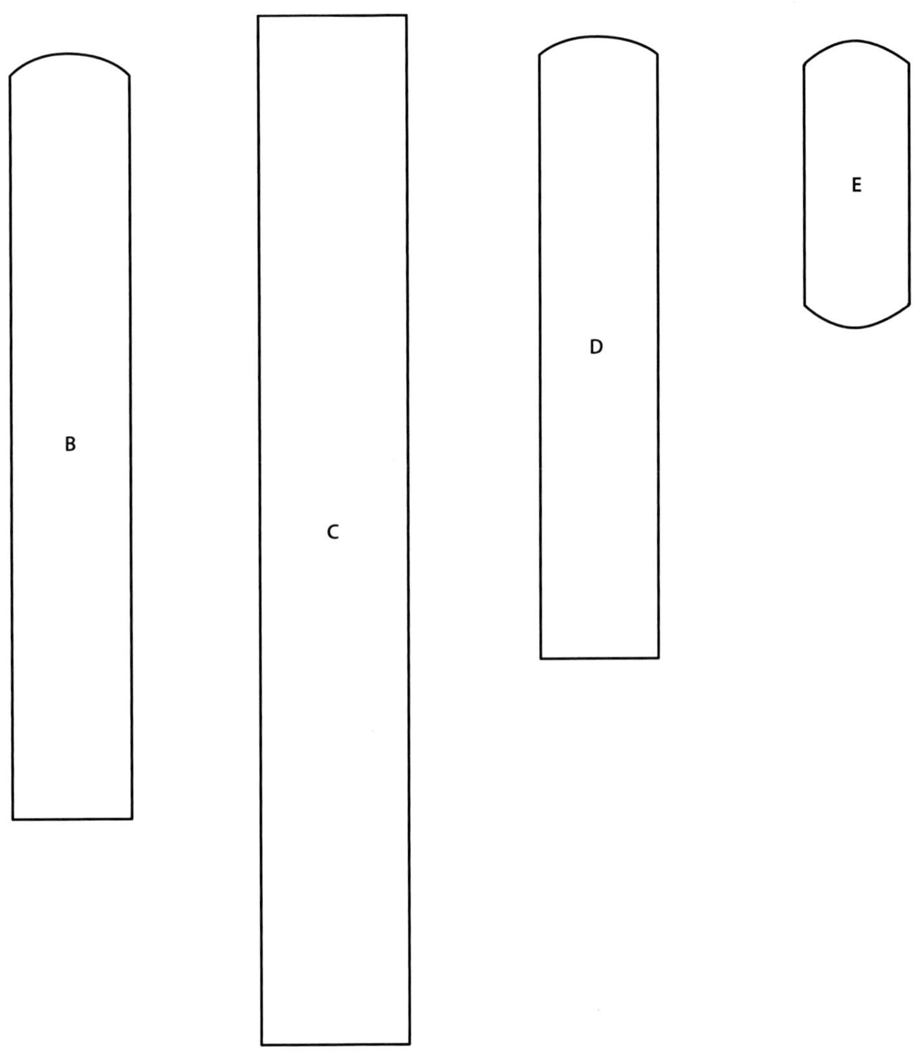
B
C
D
E

FINANCIAL DISTRICT

WHAT YOU'LL NEED

- ☐ 1 white solid strip $2^1/_2$" x 21", cut into:
  - 1 strip (A) $1^1/_2$" x $5^1/_2$".
  - 1 square (B) $2^1/_2$" x $2^1/_2$".
  - 2 rectangles (C) $2^1/_2$" x $3^1/_2$".
  - 1 rectangle (D) $2^1/_2$" x $4^1/_2$".
- ☐ 1 black/gray tone-on-tone print strip $2^1/_2$" x 21", cut into:
  - 1 square (E) $2^1/_2$" x $2^1/_2$".
  - 1 strip (F) $1^1/_2$" x $4^1/_2$".
  - 2 strips (G) 2" x $5^1/_2$".
- ☐ 1 black/white print rectangle $2^1/_2$" x 8", cut into:
  - 1 square (H) $2^1/_2$" x $2^1/_2$".
  - 1 rectangle (I) $2^1/_2$" x $4^1/_2$".

BLOCK

ASSEMBLY

*Follow **Machine Piecing**, page 86, and **Pressing**, page 87, to make block. Use a 1/4" seam allowance throughout.*

1. Sew the two C rectangles to opposite sides of the E square to make **Unit 1**.

2. Sew the D rectangle and the H square together to make **Unit 2**.

3. Join the B square and the I rectangle to make **Unit 3**.

4. Sew the A strip in between two G strips to make **Unit 4**.

5. Sew the F strip to the top of Unit 4 to make **Unit 5**.

6. Join Units 1-3 & 5 to make the **Block**.

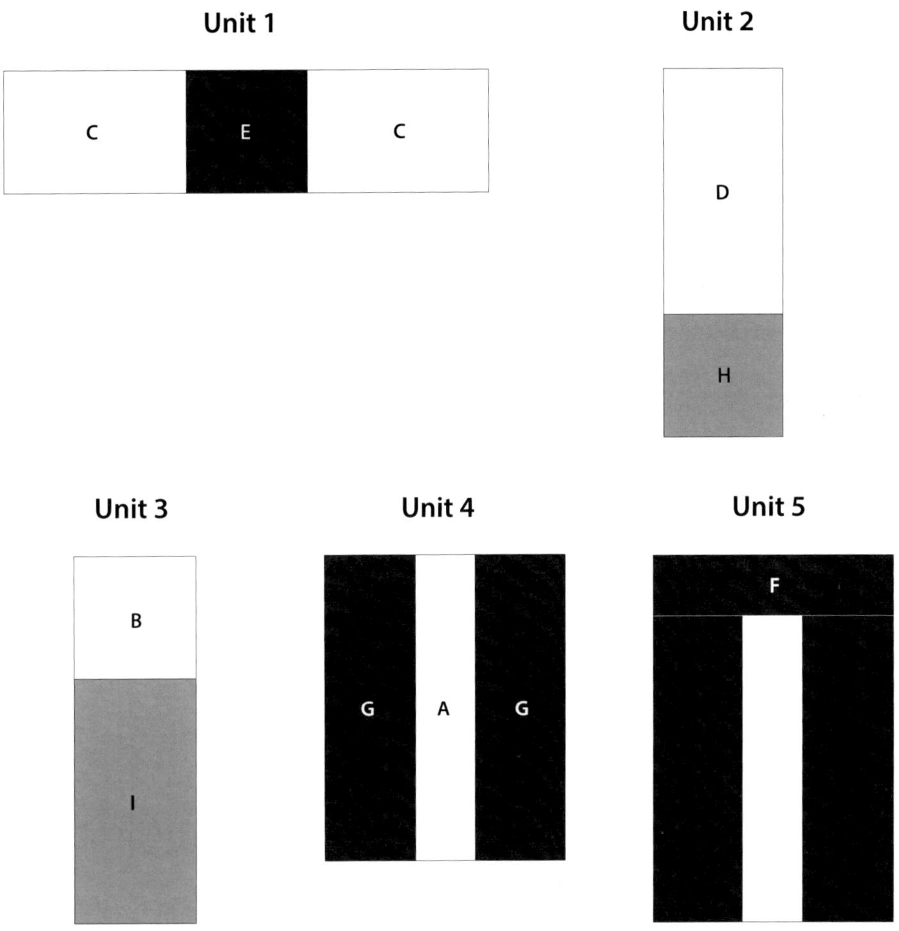

FINANCIAL DISTRICT

High rises are a distinctive feature of Financial Districts in large cities. Although their buildings' architecture may represent the Gilded age, I chose to showcase modern facades.

WATER HYDRANT

WHAT YOU'LL NEED

- ☐ 1 gray print rectangle 4 1/2" x 9"
- ☐ 1 aqua print rectangle 5 1/2" x 9"
- ☐ 1 red and white print square 6" x 6"
- ☐ 1 red tone-on-tone print square 4" x 4"

ASSEMBLY

1. Sew the rectangles together to create the background.

2. Follow **Preparing Fusible Appliqués**, page 88, and use patterns to cut appliqués.

3. Position the appliqués on the background square and fuse them according to the fusible web manufacturer's instructions.

4. Follow **Blanket Stitch Appliqué**, page 88, to appliqué pieces in place using matching thread.

5. Trim **Block** to 8 1/2" x 8 1/2".

BLOCK

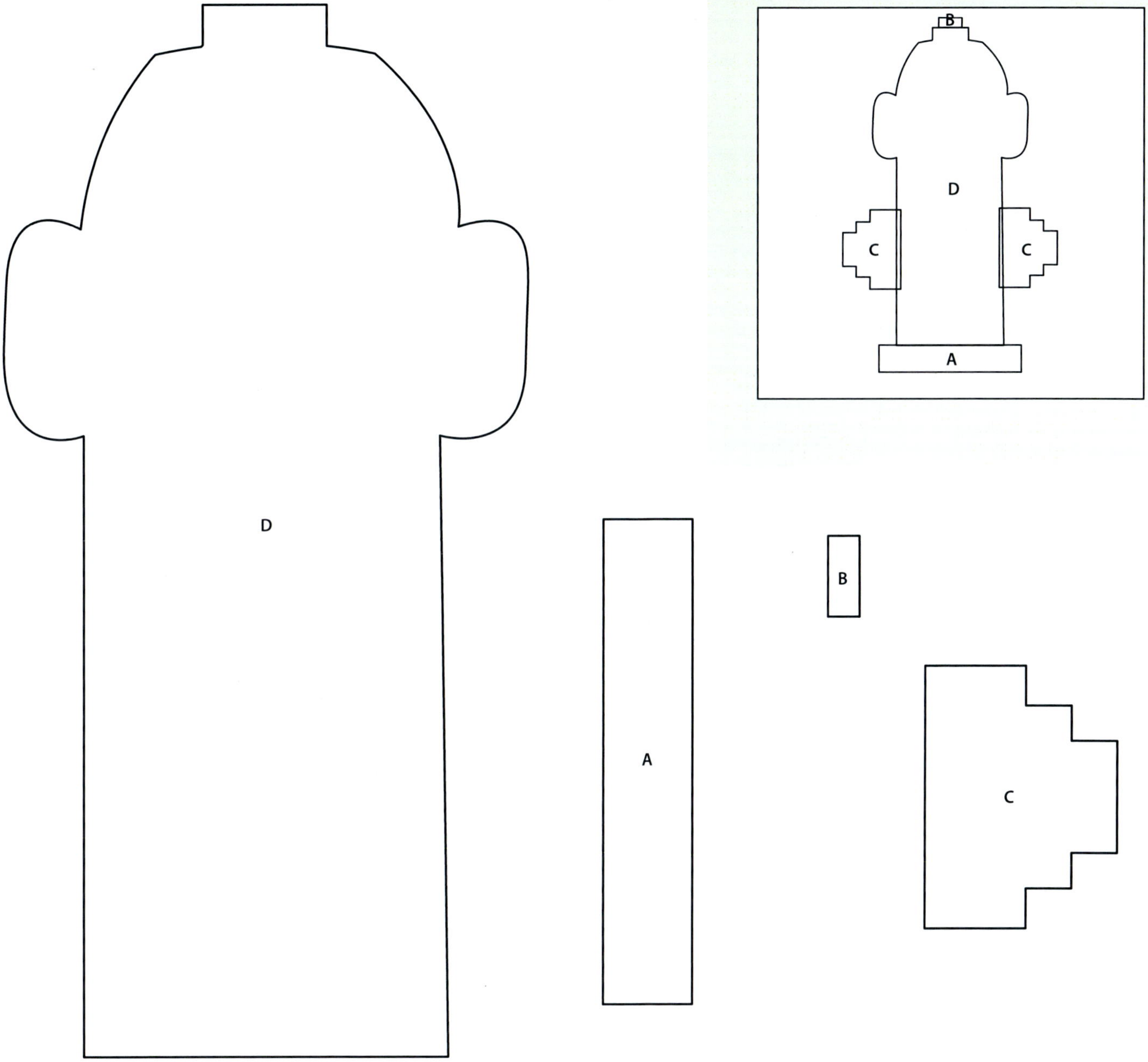

WATER HYDRANT

Hydrants are everywhere, including in children's dreams as they contemplate what to be when they grow up. I chose the iconic red hydrant, yet they can be found in many colors throughout the cities.

THE QUAD

WHAT YOU'LL NEED

- ☐ 1 green solid strip 2 1/2" x 15", cut into:
  - 5 squares 2 1/2" x 2 1/2".
- ☐ 1 purple print strip 1 1/2" x 12", cut into:
  - 4 strips 1 1/2" x 2 1/2".
- ☐ 2 white/gray strips 1 1/2" x 20", cut into:
  - 4 strips (A) 1 1/2" x 2 1/2".
  - 2 strips (B) 1 1/2" x 6 1/2".
  - 2 strips (C) 1 1/2" x 8 1/2".

ASSEMBLY

*Follow **Machine Piecing**, page 86, and **Pressing**, page 87, to make block. Use a 1/4" seam allowance throughout.*

1. Sew one purple strip to each A strip to make **Unit 1**. Make a total of 4 Unit 1's.

2. Noting fabric orientation, sew a green square in between two Unit 1's to make **Unit 2**.

3. Sew one Unit 1 in between two green squares to make **Unit 3**. Make a total of 2 Unit 3's.

4. Sew one Unit 3 to the top and one to the bottom of Unit 2 to make **Unit 4**.

BLOCK

5. Sew one B strip to each side of Unit 4 to make **Unit 5**.

6. Sew one C strip to the top and one to the bottom of Unit 5 to make the **Block**.

Unit 1 (make 4)

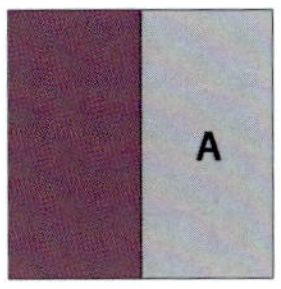

Unit 2

Unit 3 (make 2)

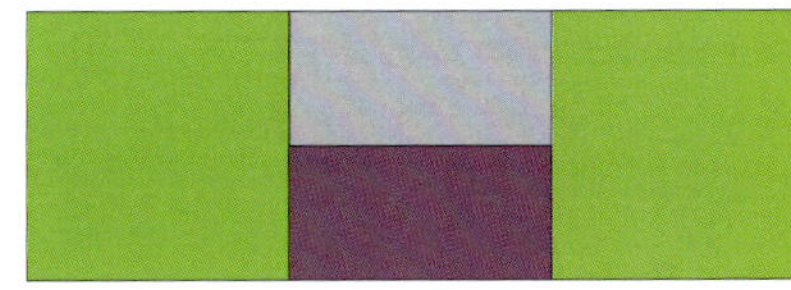

Unit 4

Unit 5

THE BOOKSTORE

WHAT YOU'LL NEED

- ☐ 4 assorted print strips $1^1/_2$" x $8^1/_2$"
- ☐ 2 assorted print strips $1^1/_2$" x $6^1/_2$"
- ☐ 1 print rectangle $2^1/_2$" x $8^1/_2$"
- ☐ 2 white solid strips $1^1/_2$" x $2^1/_2$"

ASSEMBLY

*Follow **Machine Piecing**, page 86, and **Pressing**, page 87, to make block. Use a $^1/_4$" seam allowance throughout.*

1. Sew the two white strips to the two $1^1/_2$" x $6^1/_2$" assorted print strips to make **Unit 1** & **Unit 2**.

2. Sew the strips together with Units 1 & 2 as the second and fifth books to make the **Block**.

BLOCK

Unit 1 Unit 2

THE BOOKSTORE

- Lined up with books about everything, the bookstores offer hours of enchantment to children and infinite discovery for grown-ups. I have wonderful memories of story-time at bookstores.

SMOKE STACKS

WHAT YOU'LL NEED

- ☐ 4 assorted black print rectangles 4" x 6", each cut into:
  - 1 rectangle (A) 2 1/2" x 3 1/2".
  - 1 square (B) 2 7/8" x 2 7/8".
- ☐ 1 gray print rectangle 8" x 12", cut into:
  - 4 rectangles (C) 2 1/2" x 3 1/2".
  - 4 squares (D) 2 7/8" x 2 7/8".

BLOCK

ASSEMBLY

*Follow **Machine Piecing**, page 86, and **Pressing**, page 87, to make block. Use a 1/4" seam allowance throughout.*

1. Draw a diagonal line on the wrong side of the D squares. With right sides together, layer the marked D squares atop the B squares. Stitch ¼" on each side of the marked line, cut on the drawn line to make **Unit 1**. Press each unit with seams toward dark fabric and trim dog ears. You will use only one Unit 1 of each fabric combination.
2. Noting fabric orientation, sew one C rectangle to each Unit 1 to make **Unit 2**.
3. Matching fabrics, sew the A rectangles to the bottom of Unit 2 to make **Unit 3**.
4. Sew the Unit 3's together to make the **Block**.

Unit 1
(make 4)

Unit 2
(make 4)

Unit 3 (make 4)

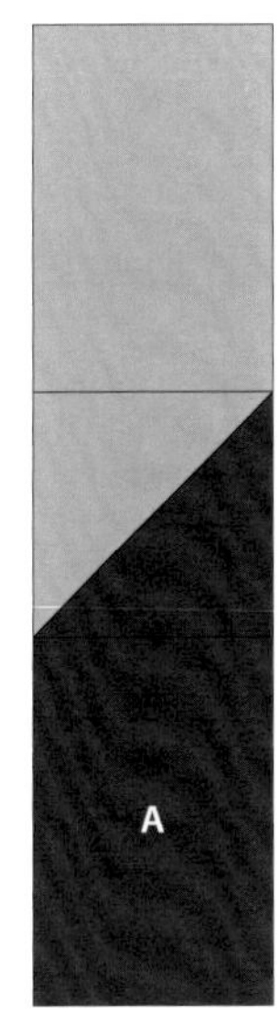

SMOKE STACKS

This block was contributed by my niece Soraia Silveira who lives in São Paulo, Brazil. I asked her for input, and she jumped right in!

THE LOFT

BLOCK

WHAT YOU'LL NEED

- ☐ 1 white solid strip 1$^1/_2$" x 36", cut into:
  - 1 strip (A) 1$^1/_2$" x 2$^1/_2$".
  - 3 strips (B) 1$^1/_2$" x 3$^1/_2$".
  - 1 strip (C) 1$^1/_2$" x 4$^1/_2$".
  - 2 strips (D) 1$^1/_2$" x 8$^1/_2$".
- ☐ 1 white solid rectangle 3$^1/_2$" x 4$^1/_2$"
- ☐ 1 green tone-on-tone print strip 1$^1/_2$" x 6", cut into:
  - 1 strip (E) 1$^1/_2$" x 3$^1/_2$".
  - 1 square (F) 1$^1/_2$" x 1$^1/_2$".
- ☐ 1 black tone-on-tone print strip 1$^1/_2$" x 8$^1/_2$"
- ☐ 1 floral print square 3$^1/_2$" x 3$^1/_2$"

ASSEMBLY

*Follow **Machine Piecing**, page 86, and **Pressing**, page 87, to make block. Use a $^1/_4$" seam allowance throughout.*

Unit 1

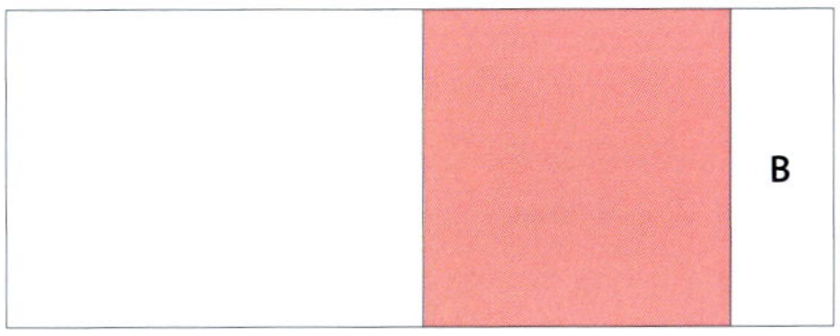

Unit 2

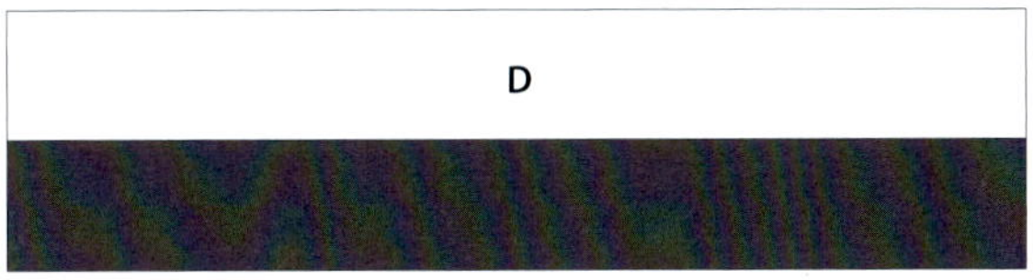

Unit 3

Unit 4

1. Sew the $3^1/_2$" x $4^1/_2$" white rectangle to the left of the floral print square and one B strip to its right to make **Unit 1**.
2. Sew one D strip and the black tone-on-tone strip together to make **Unit 2**.
3. Sew the F square in between one B strip and the C strip to make **Unit 3**.
4. Sew the E strip in between the A strip and the remaining B strip to make **Unit 4**.
5. Beginning with the remaining D strip, sew all the strips together in the order they were assembled for create the **Block**.

AT THE PLAYGROUND

WHAT YOU'LL NEED

- ☐ 1 aqua print background square 9" x 9"
- ☐ 1 black solid rectangle 5" x 7"

ASSEMBLY

1. Follow **Preparing Fusible Appliqués**, page 88, and use patterns to cut appliqués. Note: The placement of the boy and girl can easily be changed simply by changing the hair. The boy can be changed to a girl by "trimming" his hair and adding a ponytail. The girl can be changed to a boy by cutting your appliqué with tossled hair rather than a ponytail.

2. Position the appliqués on the background square, trimming the appliqués as desired. Fuse them according to the fusible web manufacturer's instructions.

3. Follow **Blanket Stitch Appliqué**, page 88, to appliqué pieces in place using matching thread.

4. Trim **Block** to $8^1/_2$" x $8^1/_2$".

BLOCK

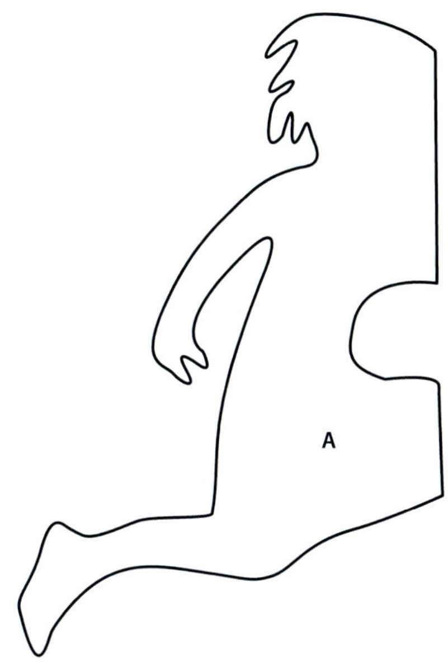

AT THE PLAYGROUND

Whether just a grassy field with a slide and a seesaw, or a large area with modern structures and sand boxes, in playgrounds children learn social skills and burn energy while parents socialize. So many memories…

GARDEN GATE

WHAT YOU'LL NEED

- ☐ 1 red floral print background square 9" x 9"
- ☐ 1 black print square $8^3/_4$" x $8^3/_4$"

ASSEMBLY

1. Follow **Preparing Fusible Appliqués**, page 88, and use pattern to cut appliqué.
2. Position the appliqué on the background square and fuse according to the fusible web manufacturer's instructions.
3. Follow **Blanket Stitch Appliqué**, page 88, to appliqué piece in place using matching thread.
4. Trim **Block** to $8^1/_2$" x $8^1/_2$".

BLOCK

TIP

When fusing the wrought iron shape, be sure to keep the iron away from the very edges of the block so the shape won't fuse to your ironing board cover. Alternately, place a mylar sheet between the ironing board and your block before fusing.

THE SCOOP

WHAT YOU'LL NEED

- ☐ 1 lime tone-on-tone print background square 9" x 9"
- ☐ 1 white/red dots print rectangle 3$^1/_2$" x 4$^1/_2$"
- ☐ 1 fuchsia print rectangle 3$^1/_2$" x 4$^1/_2$"
- ☐ 1 royal blue print square 3$^1/_2$" x 3$^1/_2$"
- ☐ 1 orange print rectangle 9" x 6"

ASSEMBLY

1. Follow **Preparing Fusible Appliqués**, page 88, and use patterns to cut appliqués.
2. Position the appliqués on the background square and fuse them according to the fusible web manufacturer's instructions.
3. Follow **Blanket Stitch Appliqué**, page 88, to appliqué pieces in place using matching thread.
4. Trim **Block** to 8$^1/_2$" x 8$^1/_2$".

BLOCK

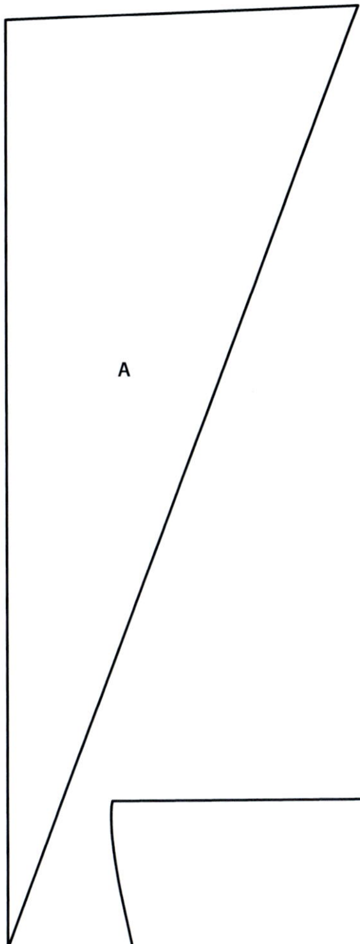

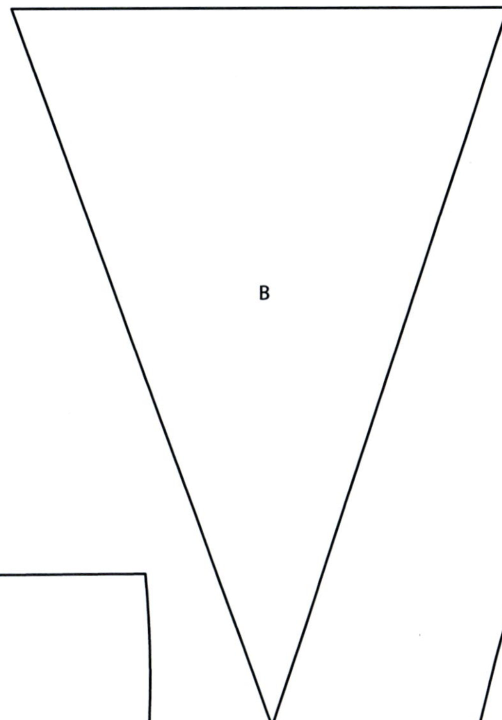

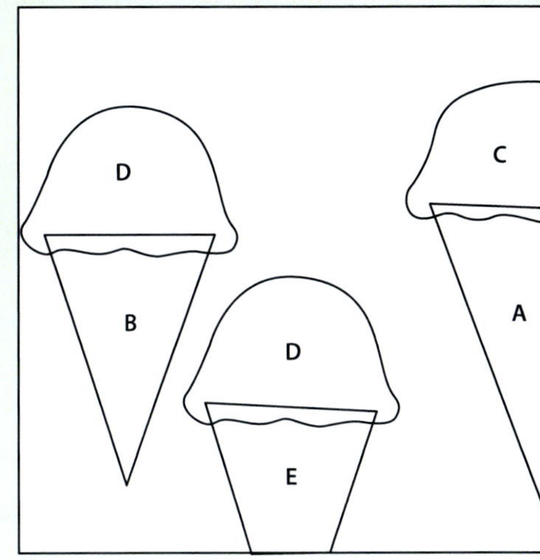

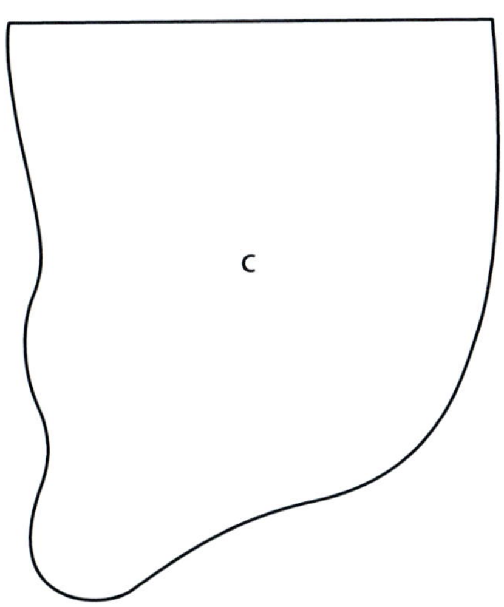

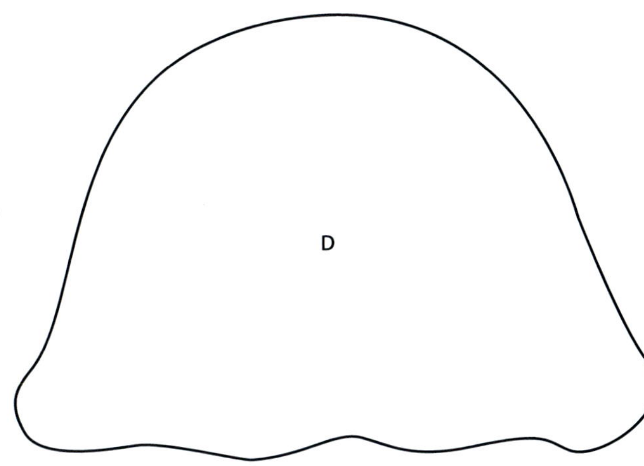

THE SCOOP

A major destination throughout the year, my city would be incomplete without an ice cream parlor. In Brazil we have Corn ice cream – my favorite! Display your favorite flavors on the block by changing the colors of the fabrics on the scoops.

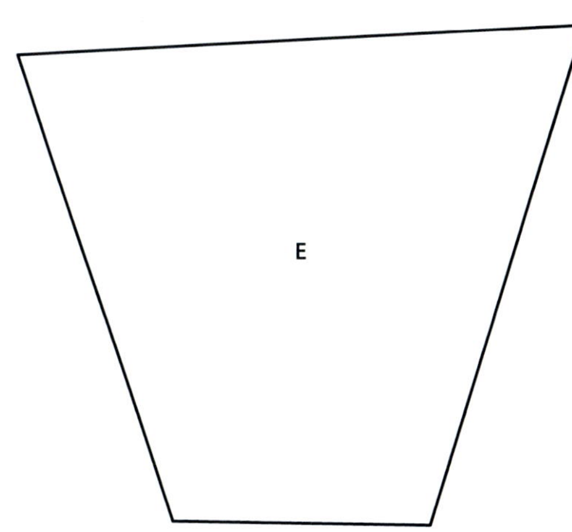

THE GYM

WHAT YOU'LL NEED

- ☐ 1 beige print tone-on-tone rectangle $4^1/_2$" x 9"
- ☐ 1 teal print rectangle $5^1/_2$" x 9"
- ☐ 1 black solid square $7^1/_2$" x $7^1/_2$"

ASSEMBLY

1. Sew the rectangles together to create the background.
2. Follow **Preparing Fusible Appliqués**, page 88, and use patterns to cut appliqués.
3. Position the appliqués on the background square and fuse them according to the fusible web manufacturer's instructions.
4. Follow **Blanket Stitch Appliqué**, page 88, to appliqué pieces in place using matching thread.
5. Trim **Block** to $8^1/_2$" x $8^1/_2$".

BLOCK

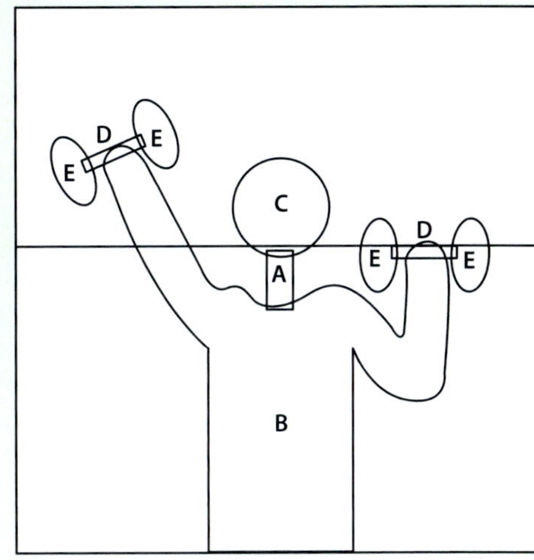

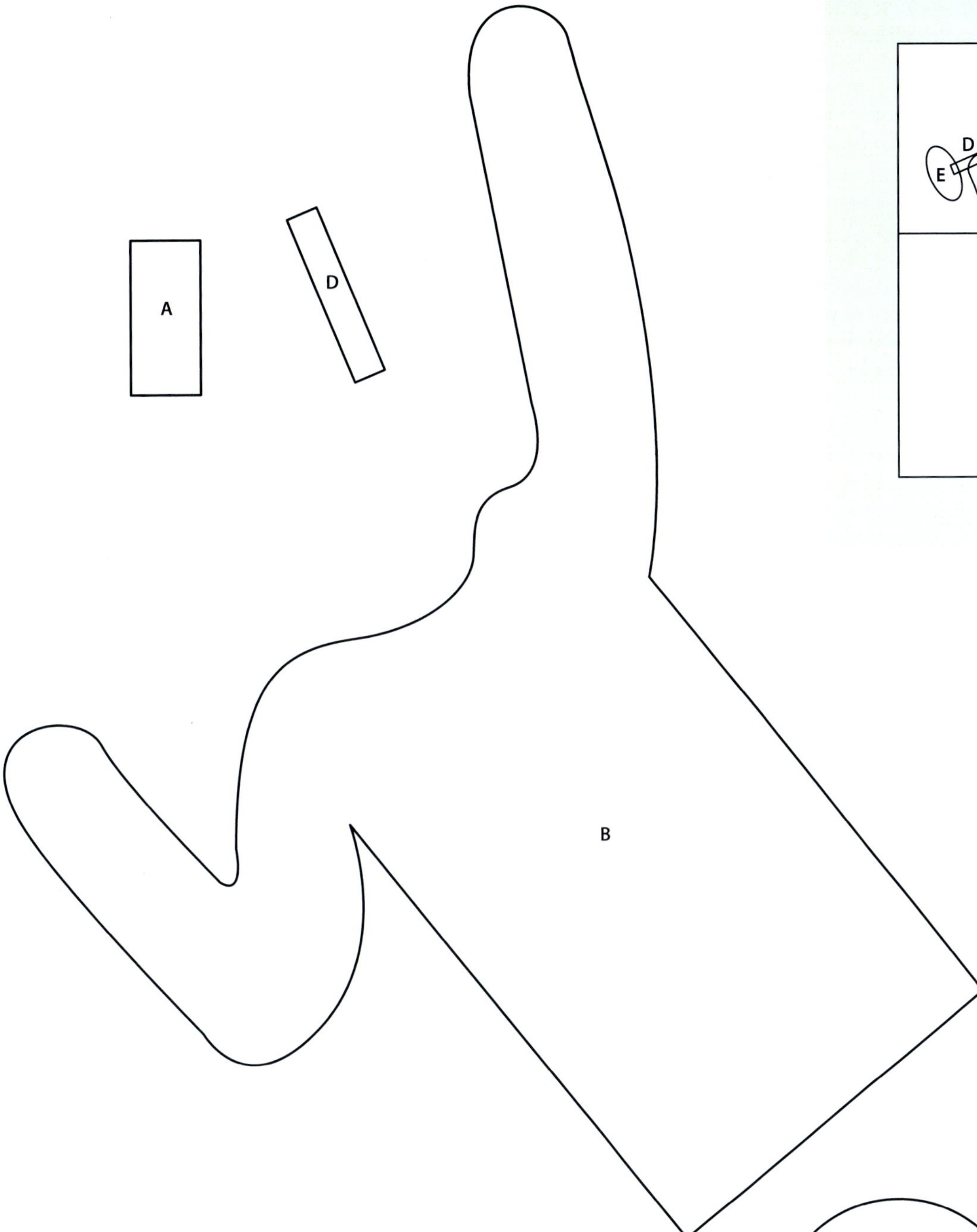

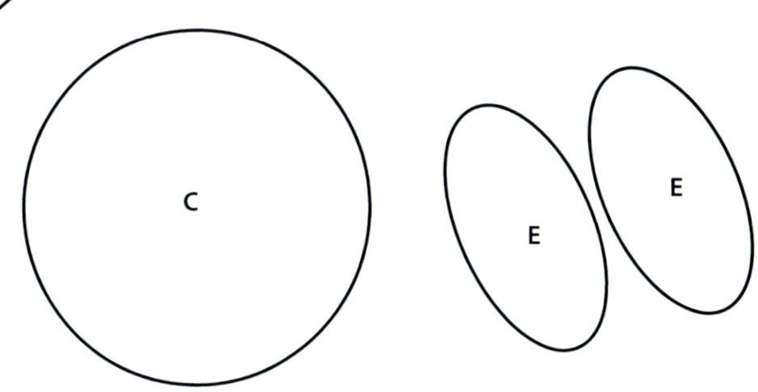

THE GYM

Gyms have become a fixture in almost every neighborhood. In our city today, we have at least six! When the outdoors are rainy, they become the perfect place to ensure last night's chocolate cake will not spend a lifetime on our hips.

COFFEE SHOP

WHAT YOU'LL NEED

- ☐ 1 gray print background square 9" x 9"
- ☐ 1 red print rectangle 4" x 5"
- ☐ scrap of dark gray solid fabric for steam

ASSEMBLY

1. Follow **Preparing Fusible Appliqués**, page 88, and use patterns to cut appliqués.
2. Position the appliqués on the background square and fuse them according to the fusible web manufacturer's instructions.
3. Follow **Blanket Stitch Appliqué**, page 88, to appliqué pieces in place using matching thread.
4. Trim **Block** to $8^1/_2$" x $8^1/_2$".

BLOCK

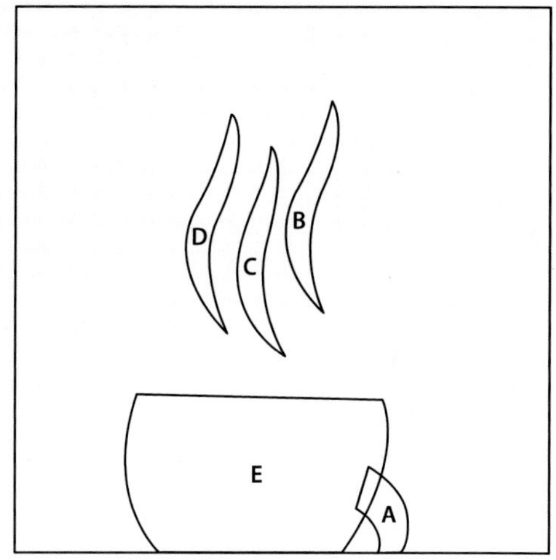

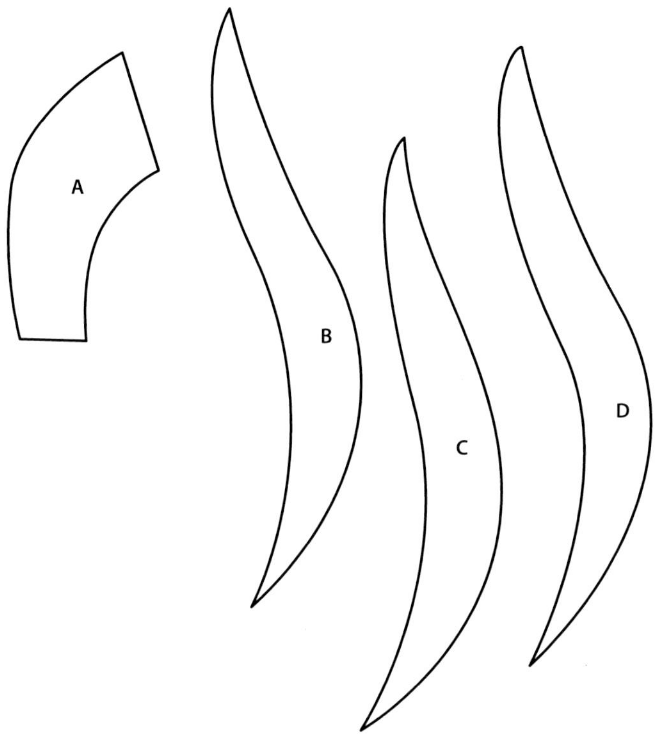

COFFEE SHOP

I like coffee and you like tea or chocolate. The corner coffee shop is a favorite gathering place in any city so it must have a spot in our quilt.

THE EATERY

WHAT YOU'LL NEED

- ☐ 1 fuchsia tone-on-tone print background square 8$^{1}/_{2}$" x 8$^{1}/_{2}$"
- ☐ 1 gray print rectangle 3$^{1}/_{2}$" x 8"
- ☐ 1 aqua print rectangle 3$^{1}/_{2}$" x 8"

ASSEMBLY

1. Follow **Preparing Fusible Appliqués**, page 88, and use patterns to cut appliqués.

2. Position the appliqués on the background square and fuse them according to the fusible web manufacturer's instructions.

3. Follow **Blanket Stitch Appliqué**, page 88, to appliqué pieces in place using matching thread.

4. Trim **Block** to 8$^{1}/_{2}$" x 8$^{1}/_{2}$".

BLOCK

THE EATERY

Many of my city memories involve celebrations at restaurants: a large family group or just with our children, sharing wonderful meals and delicious desserts. You may want to add the name of your favorite restaurant to this block!

AVIARY

WHAT YOU'LL NEED

- ☐ 1 floral print rectangle 5" x 15", cut into:
  - 1 rectangle (A) 3" x $3^1/_2$".
  - 1 rectangle (B) $2^1/_2$" x $4^1/_2$".
  - 1 rectangle (C) $4^1/_2$" x $5^1/_2$".
  - 1 rectangle (D) $3^1/_2$" x 5".
- ☐ 1 teal print strip $1^1/_2$" x 18", cut into:
  - 1 strip (E) $1^1/_2$" x $3^1/_2$".
  - 1 strip (F) $1^1/_2$" x $4^1/_2$".
  - 1 strip (G) $1^1/_2$" x $8^1/_2$".
- ☐ 1 black solid rectangle 5" x 6"

ASSEMBLY

*Follow **Machine Piecing**, page 86, and **Pressing**, page 87, to make block. Use a $^1/_4$" seam allowance throughout.*

1. Sew the E strip in between the A and the D rectangles to make **Unit 1**.
2. Sew the F strip in between the C and B rectangles to make **Unit 2**.
3. Sew the G strip in between the Unit 1 and Unit 2 to make **Unit 3**.
4. Follow **Preparing Fusible Appliqués**, page 88, and use patterns to cut appliqués.

BLOCK

5. Position the appliqués on Unit 3 and fuse them according to the fusible web manufacturer's instructions.
6. Follow **Blanket Stitch Appliqué**, page 88, to appliqué pieces in place using matching thread.

Unit 1

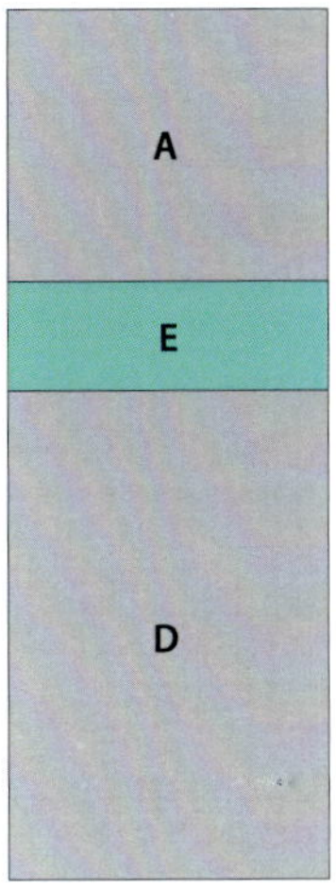

Unit 2

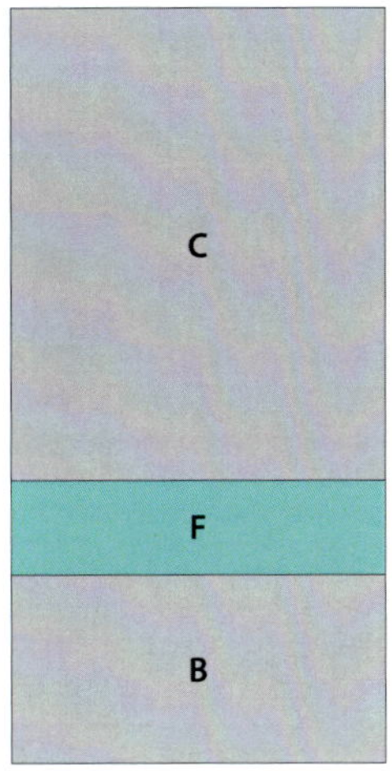

Unit 3

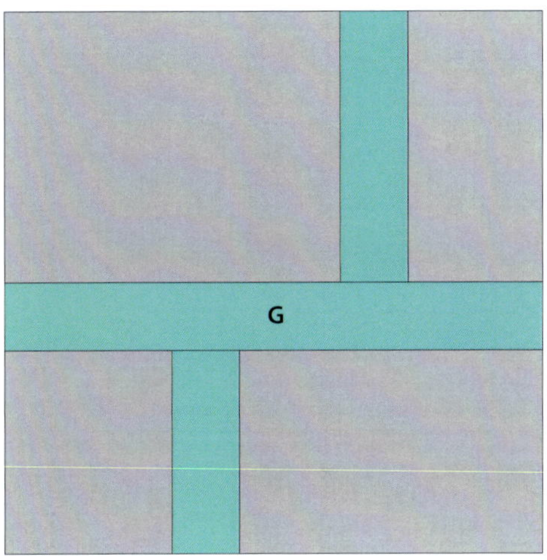

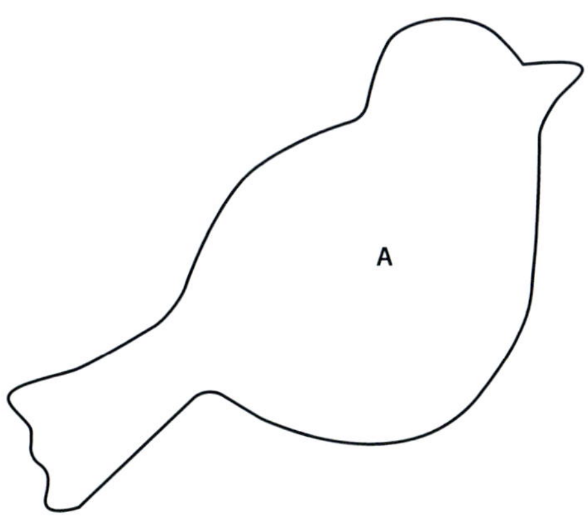

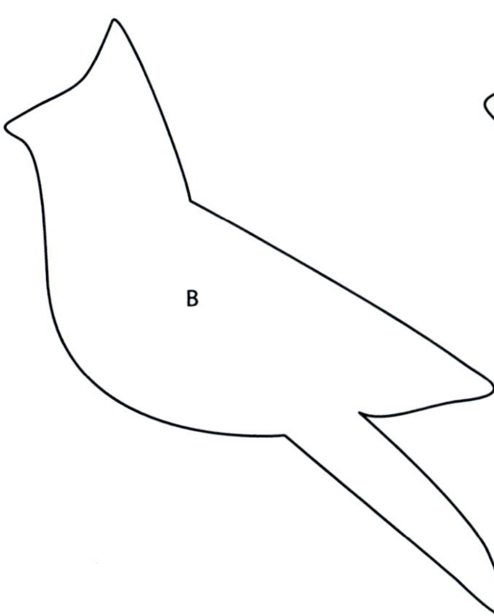

MUSEUM OF FINE ARTS

WHAT YOU'LL NEED

- ☐ 1 beige print square 10" x 10", cut into:
  - 1 strip (A) 1 1/2" x 8 1/2".
  - 1 rectangle (B) 2 1/2" x 4".
  - 1 rectangle (C) 2 1/2" x 3".
  - 2 rectangles (D) 2 1/4" x 2 1/2".
  - 2 strips (E) 1 1/2" x 3 1/2".
  - 3 squares (F) 1 1/2" x 1 1/2".
  - 2 strips (G) 1 1/2" x 2 1/2".
- ☐ 1 purple print rectangle 2 1/2" x 9", cut into:
  - 2 squares (H) 2 1/2" x 2 1/2".
  - 1 rectangle (I) 2 1/2" x 2 3/4".
- ☐ 1 black floral print rectangle 2 3/4" x 6", cut into:
  - 1 rectangle (J) 2 1/2" x 2 3/4".
  - 1 strip (K) 1 1/2" x 2 1/2".
- ☐ 1 pink tone-on-tone print strip 1 1/2" x 8", cut into:
  - 1 square (L) 1 1/2" x 1 1/2".
  - 2 strips (M) 1 1/2" x 2 1/2".

BLOCK

ASSEMBLY

*Follow **Machine Piecing**, page 86, and **Pressing**, page 87, to make block. Use a $^{1}/_{4}$" seam allowance throughout.*

1. Sew an H square in between the B and C rectanglesto make **Unit 1**.
2. Sew the D and J rectangles together to make **Unit 2**.
3. Sew the H square to the G strip to make **Unit 3**.
4. Sew one E strip to the top of the Unit 3 to make **Unit 4**.
5. Sew one M strip and one F square together **(Unit 5)** and sew this strip to the right side of Unit 4 to make **Unit 6**.
6. Sew Unit 2 to the top of the Unit 6 to make **Unit 7**.

Unit 1

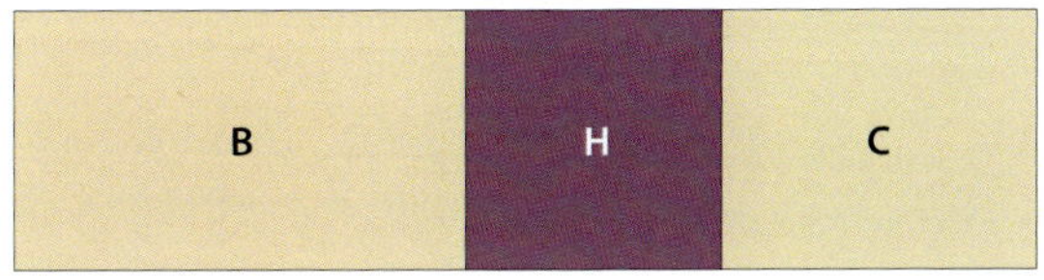

Unit 2

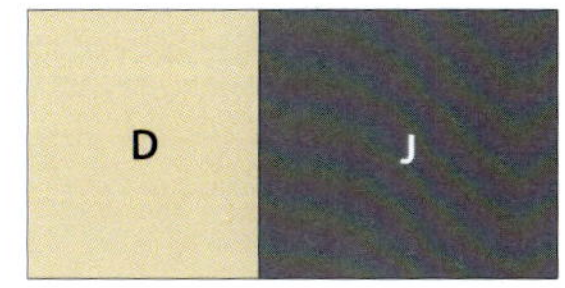

Unit 3

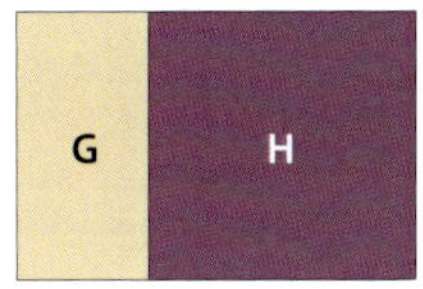

Unit 4

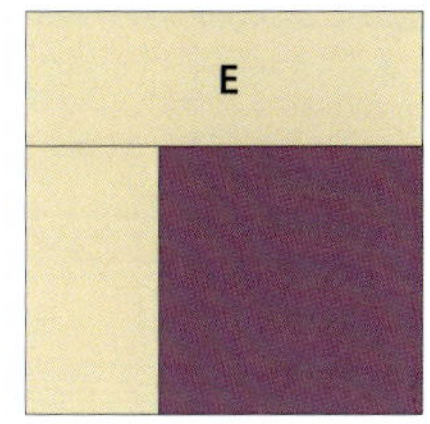

Unit 5

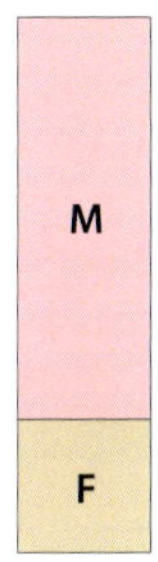

Unit 6

Unit 7

MUSEUM OF FINE ARTS

The museums in my city are breathtaking. Thus, my quilted city has one, complete with a modern installation with squares and rectangles.

7. Sew the L square and remaining E strip together **(Unit 8)**, the I and remaining D rectangles together **(Unit 9)**, and one F square on each end of an M strip **(Unit 10)**. Sew the three strips together in order to make **Unit 11**.

8. Sew the K and G strips together **(Unit 12)** and sew this unit to the bottom of the Unit 11 to make **Unit 13**.

9. Sew Unit 13 to the right side of Unit 7 to make **Unit 14**.

10. Sew the A strip to the top of the Unit 1 to make **Unit 15**.

11. Sew Unit 15 to the top of Unit 14 to create the Block.

Unit 8

Unit 9

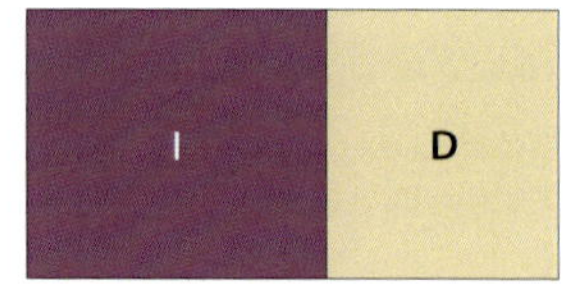

Unit 10

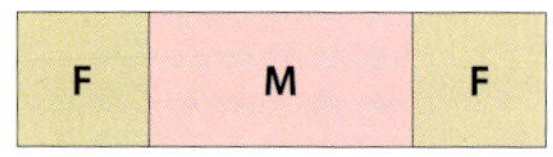

Unit 11

Unit 12

Unit 13

Unit 14

Unit 15

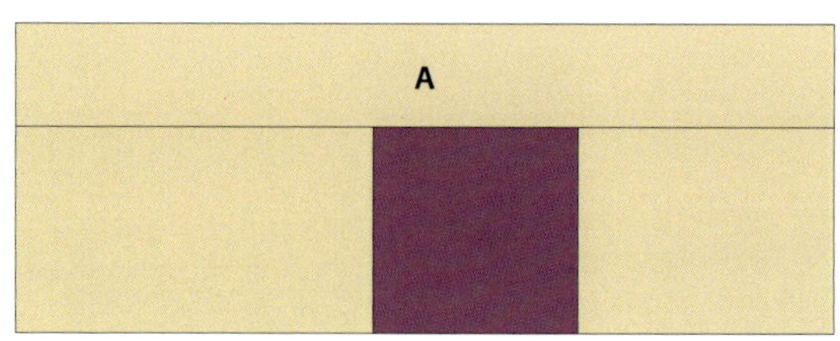

SHOW TIME

WHAT YOU'LL NEED

- ☐ 1 blue stripe background square 9" x 9"
- ☐ 1 red check print square 5" x 5"
- ☐ 1 white solid rectangle 7" x 9"

ASSEMBLY

1. Follow **Preparing Fusible Appliqués**, page 88, and use patterns to cut appliqués. Cut the box and one set of popcorn shapes on the traced line. Cut the remaining set of popcorn shapes slightly inside the traced line.

2. Position the appliqués on the background square, layering the smaller popcorn shapes under the larger popcorn shapes and fuse them according to the manufacturer's instructions.

3. Follow **Blanket Stitch Appliqué**, page 88, to appliqué pieces in place using matching thread.

4. Trim **Block** to $8^{1}/_{2}$" x $8^{1}/_{2}$".

BLOCK

TIP

Duplicating the light-colored appliqué shapes and layering them so the smaller shapes are on the bottom ensures that dark background fabrics will not show through.

B
D
C
E
A

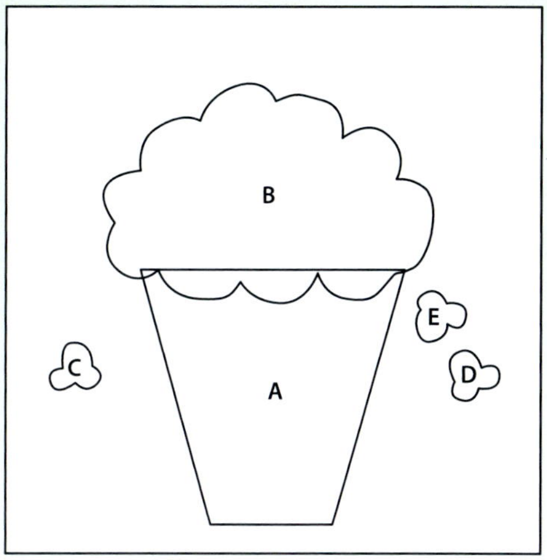
B
E
C
A
D

THE BRIDGE

WHAT YOU'LL NEED

- ☐ 1 blue print rectangle 4" x 9"
- ☐ 1 teal solid rectangle 6" x 9"
- ☐ 1 orange print rectangle 4" x 8$^{1}/_{2}$"

ASSEMBLY

1. Sew the rectangles together to create the background.
2. Follow **Preparing Fusible Appliqués**, page 88, and use patterns to cut appliqués.
3. Position the appliqués on the background square and fuse them according to the fusible web manufacturer's instructions.
4. Follow **Blanket Stitch Appliqué**, page 88, to appliqué pieces in place using matching thread.
5. Trim **Block** to 8$^{1}/_{2}$" x 8$^{1}/_{2}$".

BLOCK

TIP

The bridge parts are very narrow so cut them carefully with sharp scissors. You can use a straight stitch for the appliqué, though I like the texture the blanket stitch adds to the bridge.

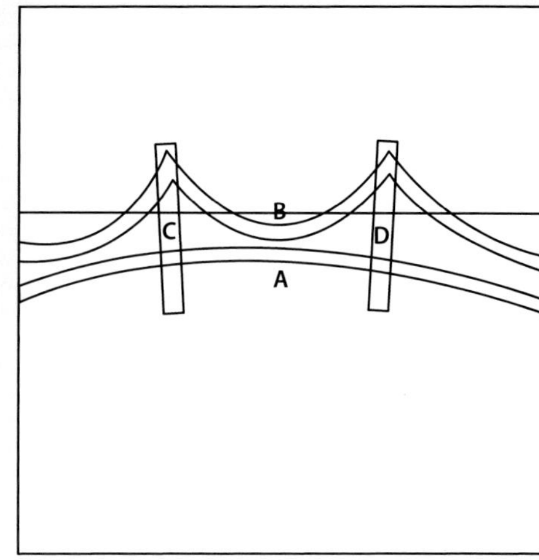
B
C
D
A

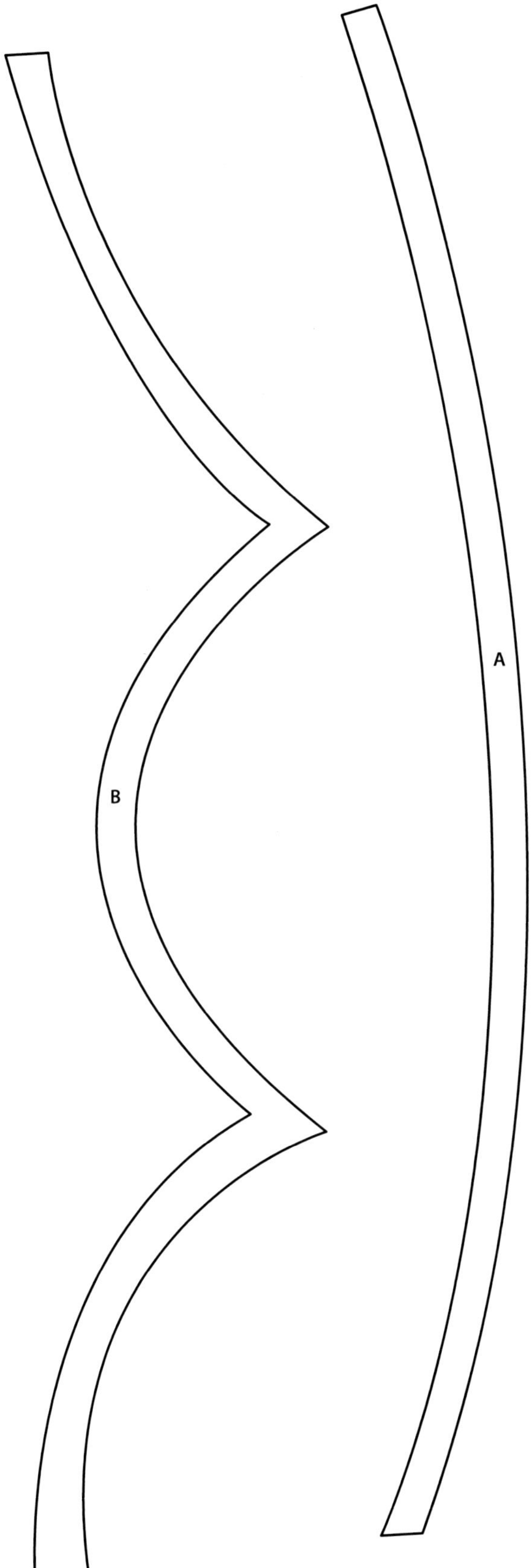
B
A

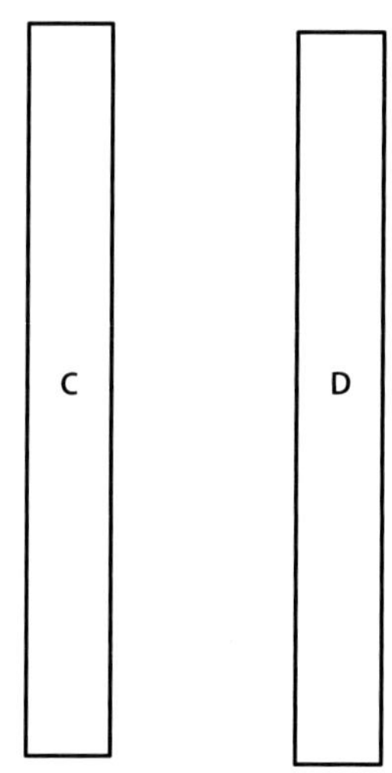
C
D

CONDOS BY THE BAY

WHAT YOU'LL NEED

- ☐ 1 teal print rectangle 6" x 11", cut into:
  - 1 strip (A) 2" x 4$^1/_2$".
  - 1 rectangle (B) 2$^1/_2$" x 5$^1/_2$".
  - 1 strip (C) 2" x 3".
  - 1 strip (D) 1$^3/_4$" x 4$^1/_2$".
  - 1 strip (E) 2$^1/_4$" x 5$^1/_2$".
- ☐ assorted print fabric strips as follows:
  - 1 strip (A1) 2" x 4$^1/_2$".
  - 1 rectangle (B1) 2$^1/_2$" x 3$^1/_2$".
  - 1 strip (C1) 2" x 6".
  - 1 strip (D1) 1$^3/_4$" x 4$^1/_2$".
  - 1 strip (E1) 2$^1/_4$" x 3$^1/_2$".

ASSEMBLY

*Follow **Machine Piecing**, page 86, and **Pressing**, page 87, to make block. Use a $^1/_4$" seam allowance throughout.*

1. Matching the letters above (A and A1, B and B1, etc.), sew fabric pieces together into two-color strips to make **Unit 1**. Make 5 Unit 1's.

2. Sew the Units together in alphabetical order to create the **Block**.

BLOCK

TIP

Decide if you want the background fabric to be the sky or the ocean and choose its color accordingly. If one is standing next to the buildings, the background is the sky, but if one is flying over them, what I see is the ocean!

CONDOS BY THE BAY

Port cities such as New York, Boston, and San Francisco often have tall buildings near the water. They inspired this block where the blue can be the water or the sky, depending on your point of view.

Unit 1

SIDEWALK

WHAT YOU'LL NEED

- ☐ 1 black/white print strip 2$^1/_2$" x 32"
- ☐ 1 white/black print strip 2$^1/_2$" x 32"
- ☐ 2 white solid strips 2$^1/_2$" x 32"
- ☐ 2$^1/_2$" square ruler or 2$^1/_2$" square template

ASSEMBLY

*Follow **Machine Piecing**, page 86, and **Pressing**, page 87, to make block. Use a $^1/_4$" seam allowance throughout.*

1. Sew a white strip to the black/white strip. Sew the remaining white strip to the white/black strips and press open.
2. Align the diagonal dashed line from 2$^1/_2$" square ruler on the seam **(Fig. 1)** and cut eight 2$^1/_2$" squares (half square triangles) from each Step 1 strip set **(Unit 1)**.
3. Noting fabric orientation and matching fabrics, sew 2 Unit 1's together to make **Unit 2** & **Unit 3**.
4. Alternating the dark and light prints, sew Unit's 2 & 3 together two at a time to make four strips **(Units 4-7)**.
5. Sew the strips together to create the **Block**.

BLOCK

TIP

A rotating mat is helpful when trimming the squares as you turn the mat around after cutting each side of the square with a rotary cutter, without having to reposition the ruler or template.

Unit 1

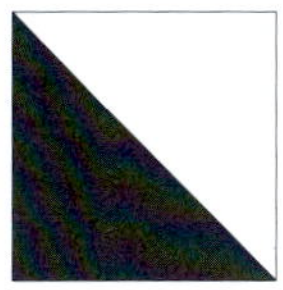

Unit 2

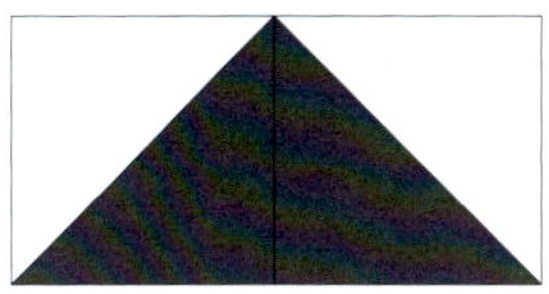

Unit 3

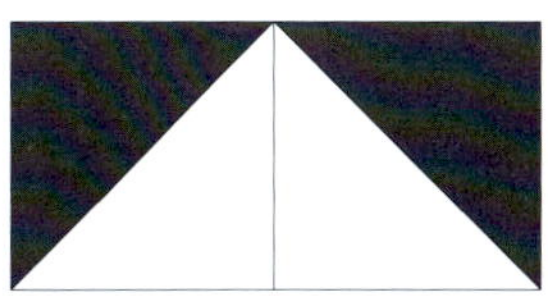

Unit 4

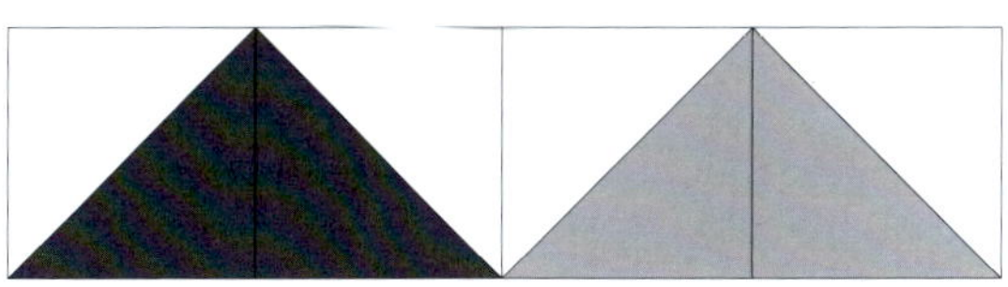

Unit 5

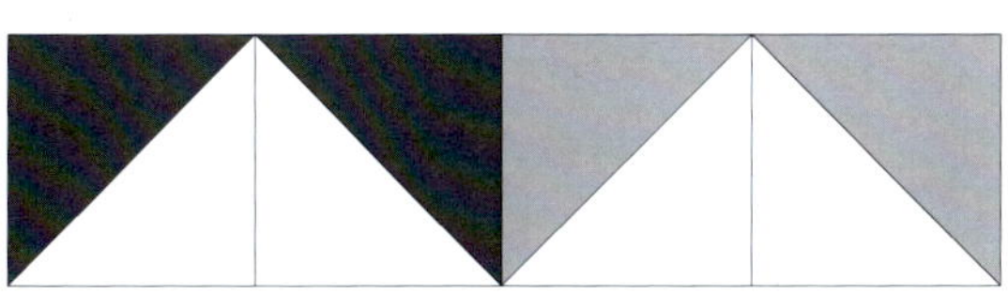

Unit 6

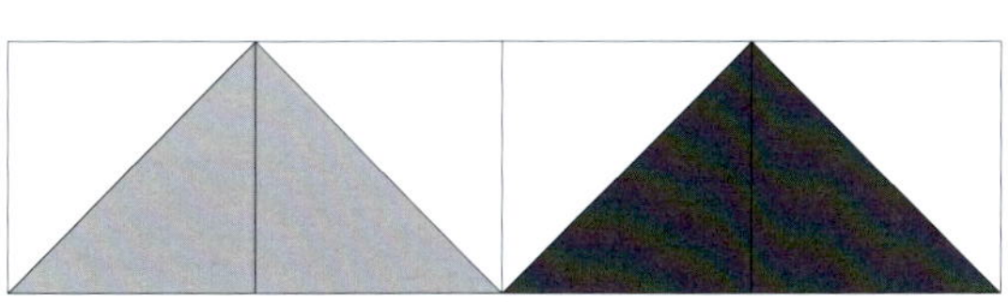

Unit 7

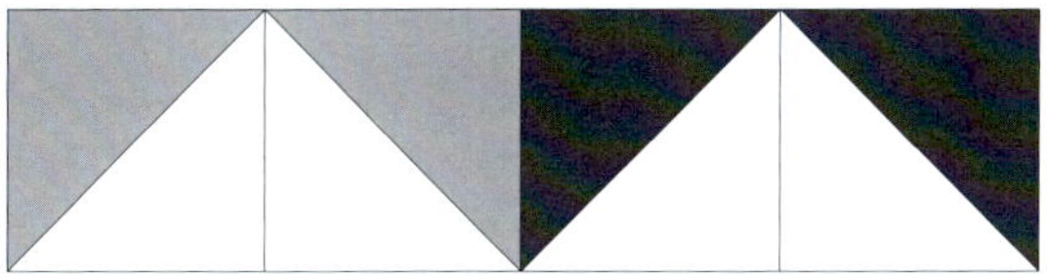

Fig. 1

BEST FRIENDS

WHAT YOU'LL NEED

- ☐ 1 blue solid square 6 1/2" x 6 1/2"
- ☐ 1 white solid rectangle 7" x 9", cut into:
  - 2 strips (A) 1 1/2" x 6 1/2".
  - 2 strips (B) 1 1/2" x 8 1/2".
- ☐ 1 black solid rectangle 4 1/2" x 6 1/2"

ASSEMBLY

1. Sew the A strips to opposite sides of the blue square to make **Unit 1**.
2. Sew the B strips to the top and bottom of the Unit 1 to make **Unit 2**.
3. Follow **Preparing Fusible Appliqués**, page 88, and use patterns to cut appliqués.
4. Position the appliqués on the 'window sill' and fuse them according to the fusible web manufacturer's instructions.
5. Follow **Blanket Stitch Appliqué**, page 88, to appliqué pieces in place using matching thread.

BLOCK

Unit 1

Unit 2

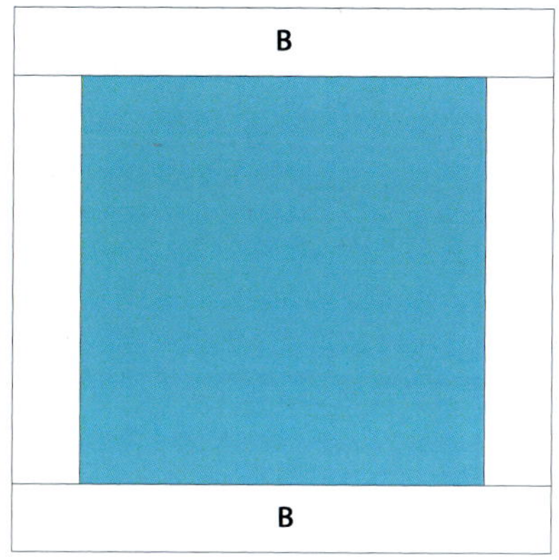

BEST FRIENDS

In the city we meet people who may become our lifelong friends. Some of them may become our best friends. I love and have had both cats and dogs. They appear side by side on this block because sometimes the best of friends may even come from different species!

THE COMMONS

WHAT YOU'LL NEED

- ☐ 1 green mottled print background square 9" x 9"
- ☐ 1 black print rectangle 4" x 5"
- ☐ 1 white solid rectangle 2" x 3"
- ☐ 1 gray print rectangle 3" x 6"

ASSEMBLY

1. Follow **Preparing Fusible Appliqués**, page 88, and use patterns to cut appliqués. Trace the light bulb twice.

2. Position the appliqués on the background square, layering the light bulb pieces, and fuse them according to the fusible web manufacturer's instructions.

3. Follow **Blanket Stitch Appliqué**, page 88, to appliqué pieces in place using matching thread; you may choose to use a straight stitch for the light post as it is a very narrow piece.

4. Trim **Block** to 8½" x 8½".

BLOCK

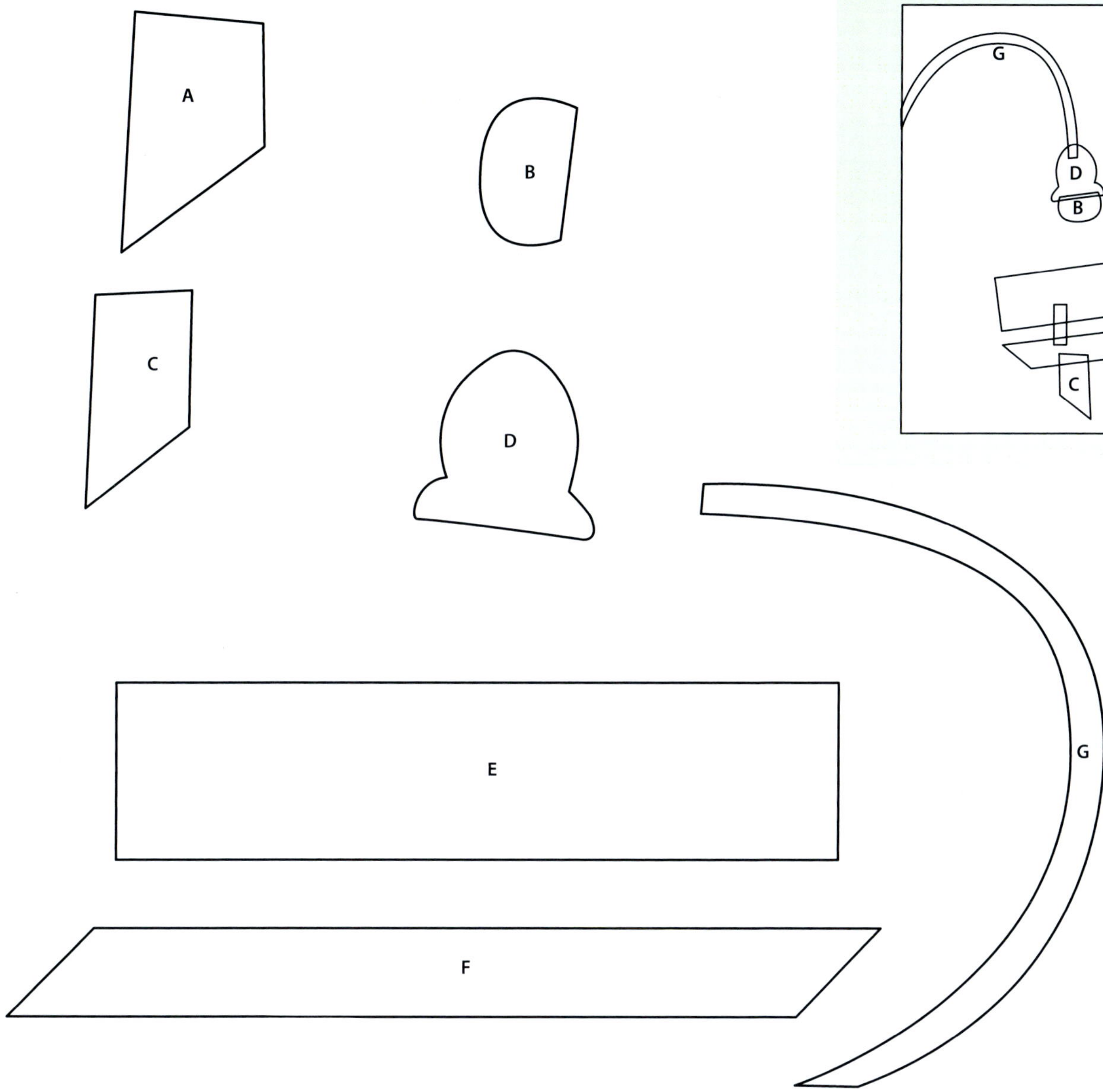

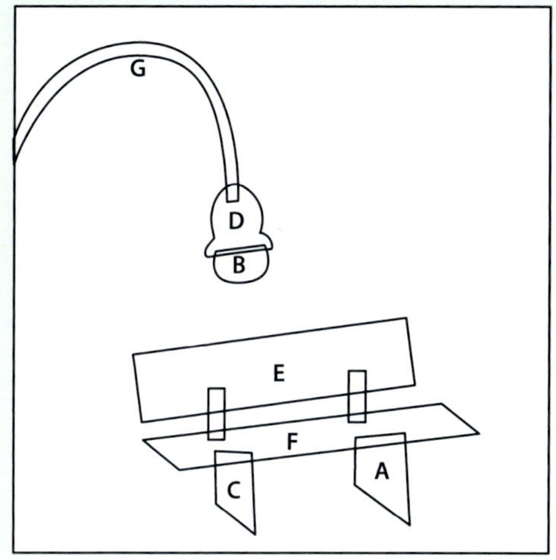

THE COMMONS

There are more than 100 parks in the city of São Paulo. Their benches have always attracted me: wood or metal, simple or ornate, covered or not but always beckoning me to pull out my book and sit for a spell.

CATHEDRAL WINDOW

WHAT YOU'LL NEED

- ☐ 1 cream print background square 9" x 9"
- ☐ 1 black print square 9" x 9"

ASSEMBLY

1. Follow **Preparing Fusible Appliqués**, page 88, and use pattern to cut appliqués.

2. Position the appliqué on the background square and fuse them according to the fusible web manufacturer's instructions. Trim the appliqué edges.

3. Follow **Blanket Stitch Appliqué**, page 88, to appliqué pieces in place using matching thread.

4. Trim **Block** to 8½" x 8½".

BLOCK

CATHEDRAL WINDOW

One distinctive feature of cathedrals, their windows with intricate stained glass designs, has always caught my eyes. I rendered their light and beauty with appliqué lines over a background square.

BOTANICAL GARDENS

WHAT YOU'LL NEED

- ☐ 1 green floral print background square 9" x 9"
- ☐ 1 pink print square 8" x 8"
- ☐ orange print scraps for flower centers

ASSEMBLY

1. Follow **Preparing Fusible Appliqués**, page 88, and use patterns to cut appliqués.
2. Position the appliqués on the background square and fuse them according to the fusible web manufacturer's instructions.
3. Follow **Blanket Stitch Appliqué**, page 88, to appliqué pieces in place using matching thread.
4. Trim **Block** to $8^1/_2$" x $8^1/_2$".

BLOCK

Achieve a soft hand on the blocks with large appliqués by cutting out some of the fusible web from inside before fusing to fabric, leaving about $^1/_4$" inside the traced line so large shapes will be hollow.

D
E
A
C
B
A
C
D
B
E

SUBWAY

WHAT YOU'LL NEED

- ☐ 1 black and white print strip $1\frac{1}{2}$" x 24", cut into:
  - 6 strips (A)$1\frac{1}{2}$" x $2\frac{1}{2}$".
  - 2 strips (B) $1\frac{1}{2}$" x $3\frac{1}{2}$".
- ☐ 1 rose print strip $1\frac{1}{2}$" x 17", cut into:
  - 3 strips (C) $1\frac{1}{2}$" x $2\frac{1}{2}$".
  - 2 strips (D) $1\frac{1}{2}$" x $3\frac{1}{2}$".
- ☐ 1 lime green print rectangle $2\frac{1}{2}$" x 25", cut into:
  - 8 squares (E) $2\frac{1}{2}$" x $2\frac{1}{2}$".
  - 1 strip (F) $1\frac{1}{2}$" x $2\frac{1}{2}$".

BLOCK

ASSEMBLY

*Follow **Machine Piecing**, page 86, and **Pressing**, page 87, to make block. Use a $\frac{1}{4}$" seam allowance throughout.*

1. Sew the following fabric pieces (E, A, E, C, & E) together in this order to make **Unit 1**. Make 2 Unit 1's.
2. Sew one D strip in between one B strip and one A strip to make **Unit 2**. Repeat to make two Unit 2's.
3. Sew the remaining strips (A, E, C, E, A, & F) together in this order to make **Unit 3**.
4. Sew one Unit 2 to the top and one to the bottom of Unit 3 to make **Unit 4**.
5. Sew one Unit 1 to the top and one to the bottom of Unit 4 to complete the **Block**.

Unit 1 (make 2)

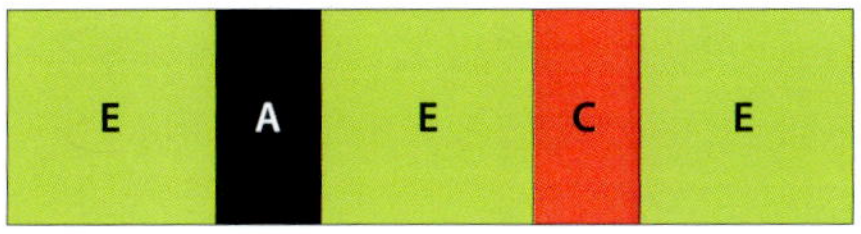

Unit 2 (make 2)

Unit 3

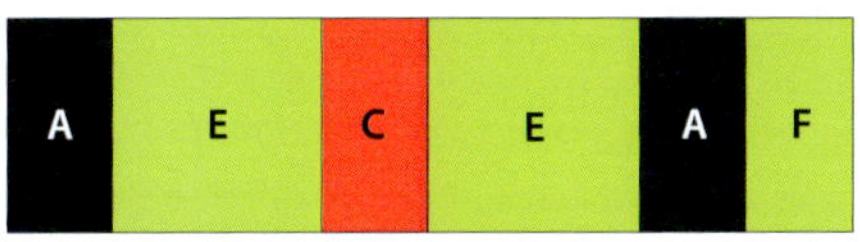

Unit 4

SUBWAY

An indispensable mode of transportation in large cities, the subway maps inspired this block with their colorful grids.

TRAIN STATION

WHAT YOU'LL NEED

- ☐ 1 dark gray print rectangle 2½" x 5½"
- ☐ 1 rose print rectangle 5½" x 6"
- ☐ 1 gray tone-on-tone print background square 9" x 9"
- ☐ scraps of yellow print fabric for lights
- ☐ scrap of white solid for the destination sign

ASSEMBLY

1. Follow **Preparing Fusible Appliqués**, page 88, and use patterns to cut appliqués.
2. Position the appliqués on the background square and fuse them according to the fusible web manufacturer's instructions.
3. Follow **Blanket Stitch Appliqué**, page 88, to appliqué pieces in place using matching thread.
4. Use the fabric marker to write the word "South" on the destination box.
5. Trim **Block** to 8½" x 8½".

BLOCK

Note: This block uses reverse appliqué, as you will blanket stitch inside the train window. Reverse appliqué is easy when done by machine!

TIP

Customize this block by substituting your favorite destination for the word "South". The box may need to be lengthened to accommodate the new word(s).

B

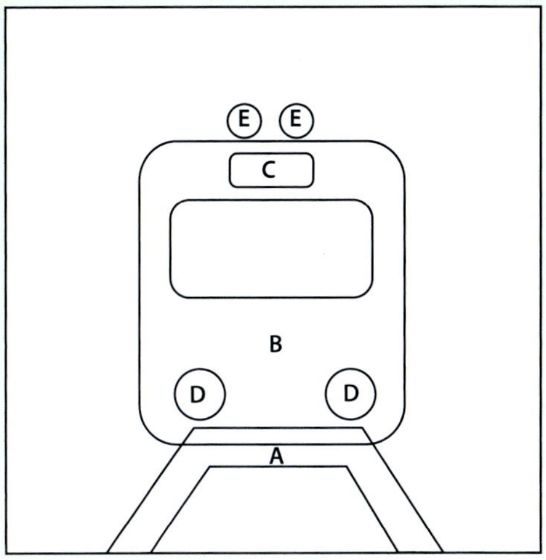
E
E
C
B
D
D
A

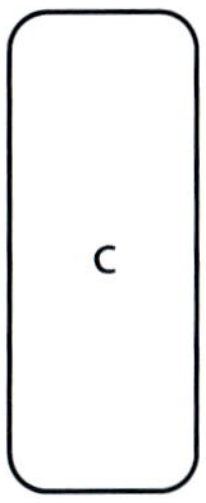
C

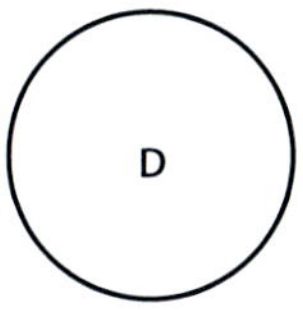
D

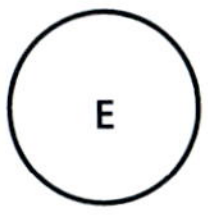
E

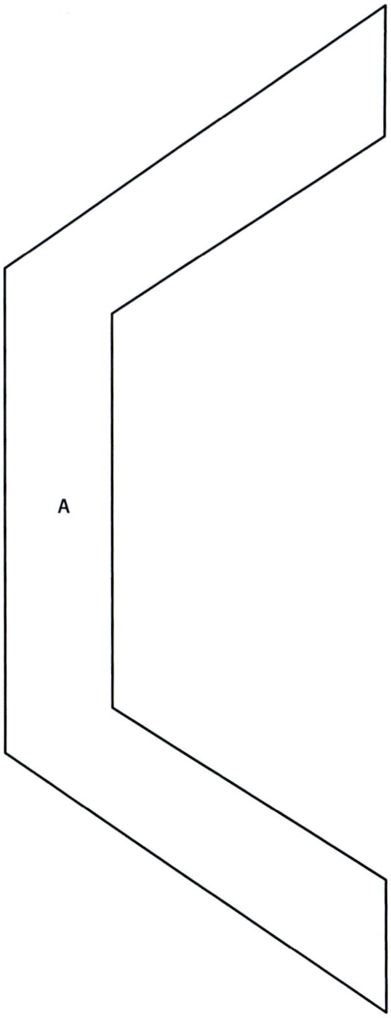
A

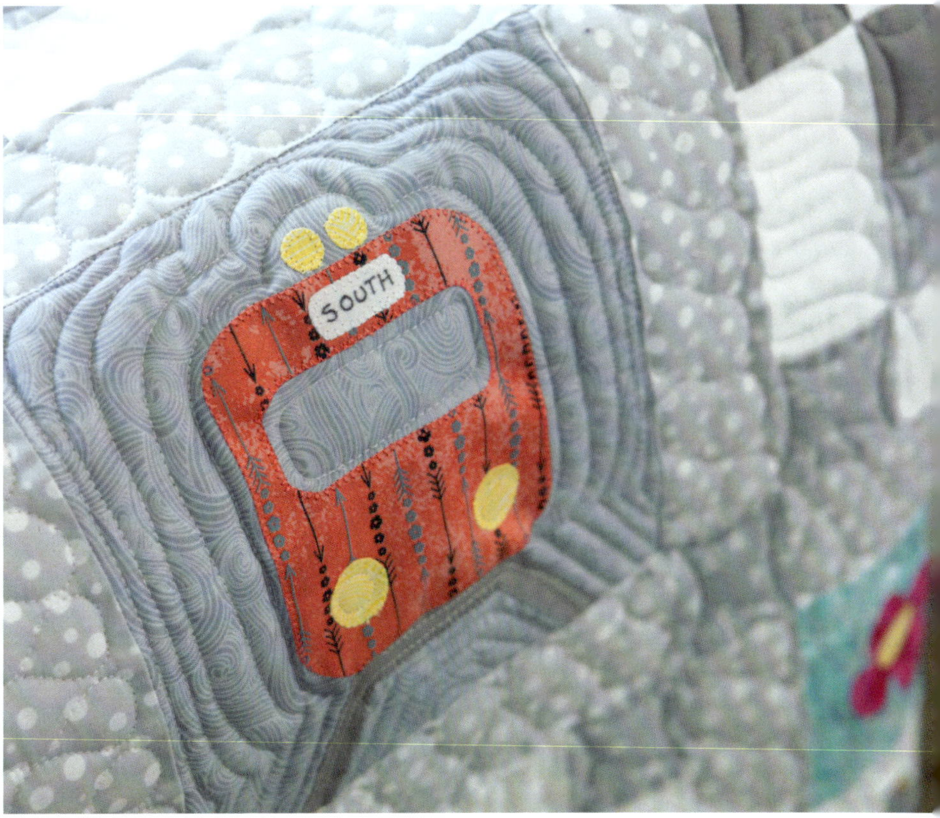
SOUTH

BUS STOP

BLOCK

WHAT YOU'LL NEED

- ☐ 1 mottled gray print rectangle 6" x 9"
- ☐ 1 gray/teal print rectangle 4" x 9"
- ☐ 1 black solid strip $1\frac{1}{2}$" x 7"
- ☐ 1 purple print rectangle 3" x 6"
- ☐ 1 teal solid square 3" x 3"

ASSEMBLY

*Follow **Machine Piecing**, page 86, and **Pressing**, page 87, to make block. Use a $\frac{1}{4}$" seam allowance throughout.*

1. Sew the mottled gray and the gray/teal rectangles together to form the background.
2. Follow **Preparing Fusible Appliqués**, page 88, and use patterns to cut appliqués.
3. Position the appliqués on the background square and fuse them according to the fusible web manufacturer's instructions.
4. Follow **Blanket Stitch Appliqué**, page 88, to appliqué pieces in place using matching thread.
5. Use fabric marker to write the words "Bus Stop" on the sign.
6. Trim **Block** to $8\frac{1}{2}$" x $8\frac{1}{2}$".

A

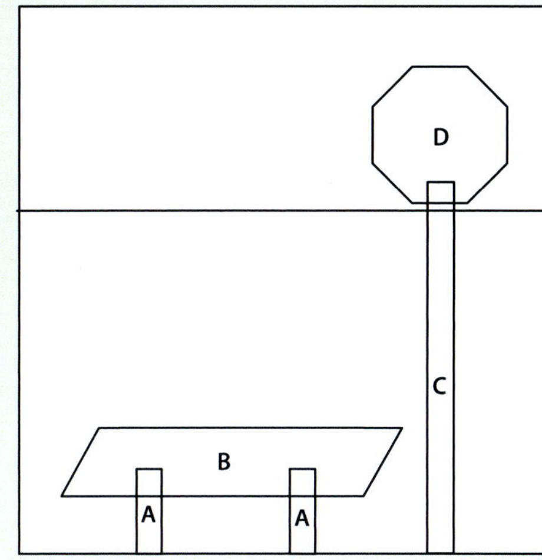

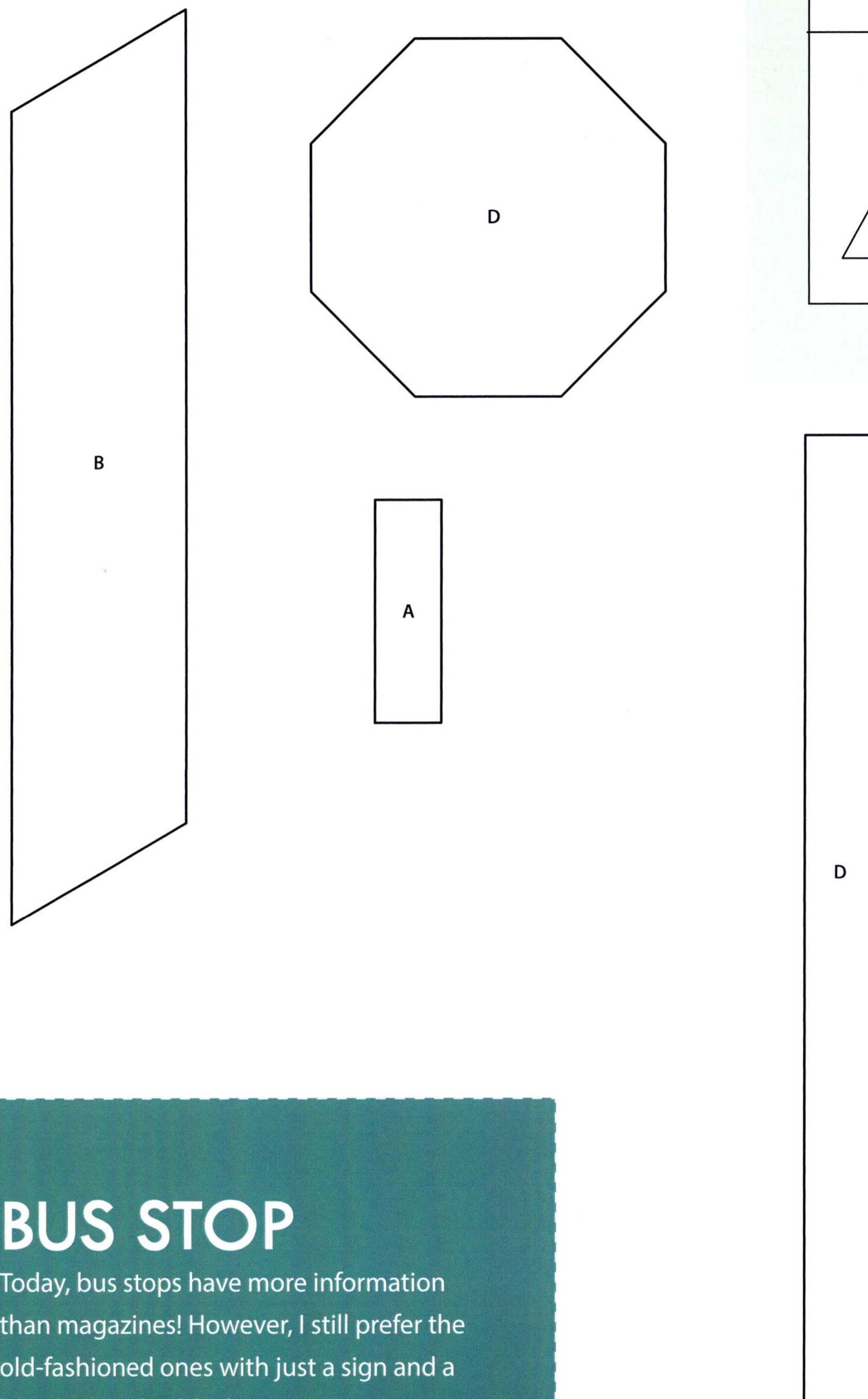

BUS STOP

Today, bus stops have more information than magazines! However, I still prefer the old-fashioned ones with just a sign and a bench as in this block.

FLY AWAY

WHAT YOU'LL NEED

- ☐ 1 blue tone-on-tone print background square 9" x 9"
- ☐ 1 gray print rectangle 7" x 4$^{1}/_{2}$"

ASSEMBLY

1. Follow **Preparing Fusible Appliqués**, page 88, and use patterns to cut appliqués.
2. Position the appliqués on the background square and fuse them according to the fusible web manufacturer's instructions.
3. Follow **Blanket Stitch Appliqué**, page 88, to appliqué pieces in place using matching thread.
4. Trim **Block** to 8$^{1}/_{2}$" x 8$^{1}/_{2}$".

BLOCK

FLY AWAY

I used to think that a town could only be called a city if it had an airport and lots of airplanes going in and out of it. Supersonic airplanes where part of my childhood as I lived for many years very close to a military airbase in the center of Brazil.

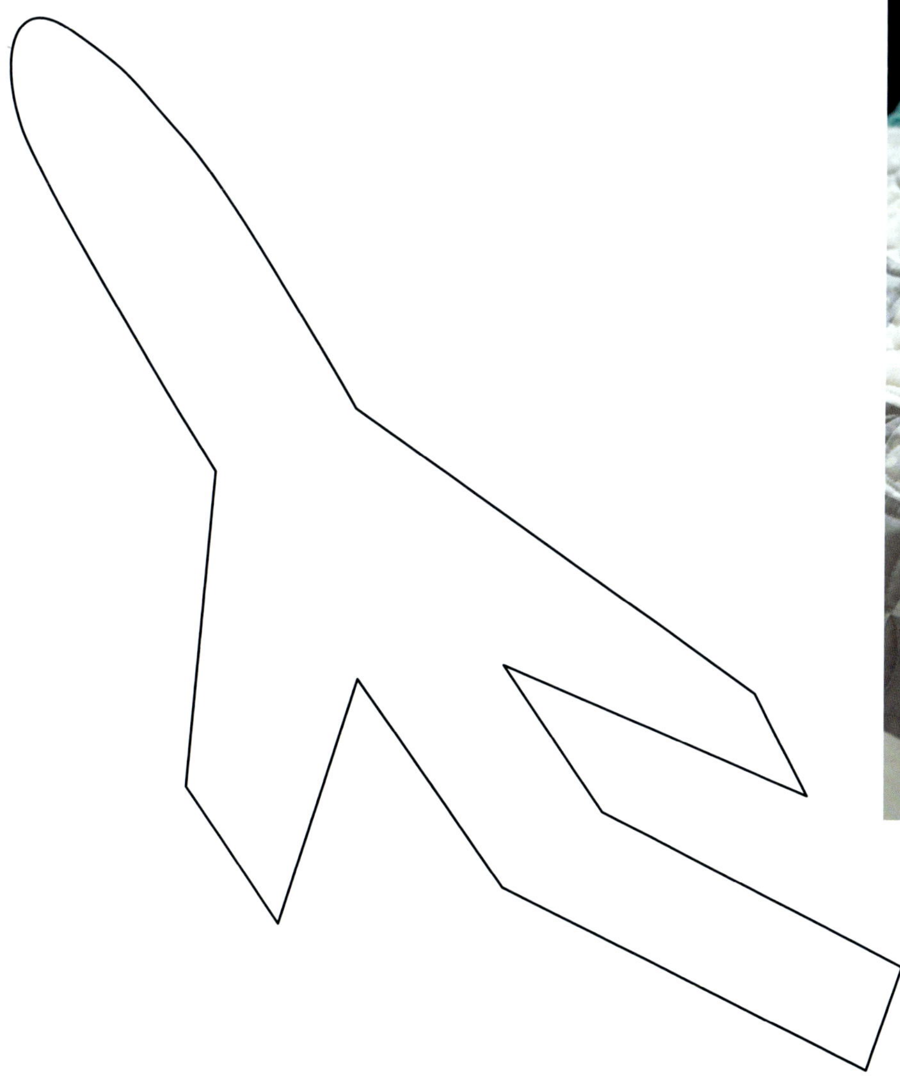

POOL TILES

WHAT YOU'LL NEED

- ☐ 1 royal blue print rectangle 8" x 14" cut into:
  - 2 squares (A) 4 1/2" x 4 1/2".
  - 8 squares (B) 1 1/2" x 1 1/2".
  - 2 circles (C) 1 1/8" diameter
- ☐ 1 orange tone-on-tone print rectangle 9" x 22", cut into:
  - 2 squares (E) 4 1/2" x 4 1/2".
  - 8 squares (D) 2 1/2" x 2 1/2".

ASSEMBLY

*Follow **Machine Piecing**, page 86, and **Pressing**, page 87, to make block. Use a 1/4" seam allowance throughout.*

1. Draw a diagonal line on the wrong side of the B squares. With right sides together, place one marked B square on each corner of one E square and stitch on the drawn line. Trim seam allowances **(Fig. 1)** to 1/4" and press open to make **Unit 1**. Repeat with the remaining B and E squares to make another Unit 1.

2. Follow **Preparing Fusible Appliqué**, page 88, and use pattern to cut circle appliqué.

3. Position one circle appliqué on each Unit 1 and fuse them according to the fusible web manufacturer's instructions.

BLOCK

4. Follow **Blanket Stitch Appliqué**, page 88, to appliqué circles in place using matching thread.

5. Draw a diagonal line on the wrong side of the D squares. Repeat Step 1 using A squares and D squares to make a **Unit 2**. Make a total of 2 Unit 2's.

6. Sew the Unit 1's and Unit 2's together to make **Units 3** & **Unit 4**. Sew Units 3 & 4 together to make the **Block**.

Fig. 1

Unit 1

Unit 2

Unit 3

Unit 4

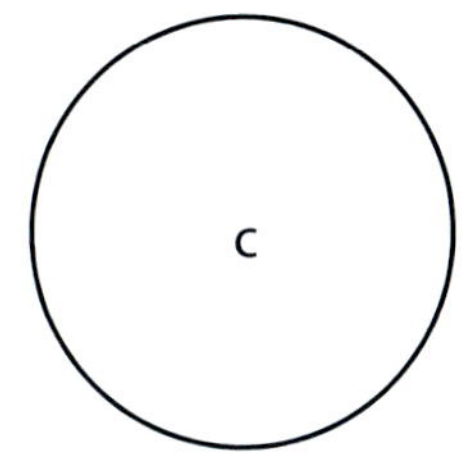

THE MARKET

WHAT YOU'LL NEED

- ☐ 2 white solid squares 5" x 5"
- ☐ 2 aqua print squares 5" x 5"
- ☐ scraps of pink, yellow, orange, red, green, and floral print fabrics

ASSEMBLY

*Follow **Machine Piecing**, page 86, and **Pressing**, page 87, to make block. Use a 1/4" seam allowance throughout.*

1. Sew the white and aqua squares together to create a **4-Patch Unit**.
2. Follow **Preparing Fusible Appliqués**, page 88, and use patterns to cut appliqués.
3. Position the appliqués on the 4-Patch Unit and fuse them according to the fusible web manufacturer's instructions.
4. Follow **Blanket Stitch Appliqué**, page 88, to appliqué pieces in place using matching thread.
5. Trim **Block** to 8 1/2" x 8 1/2".

BLOCK

4-Patch Unit

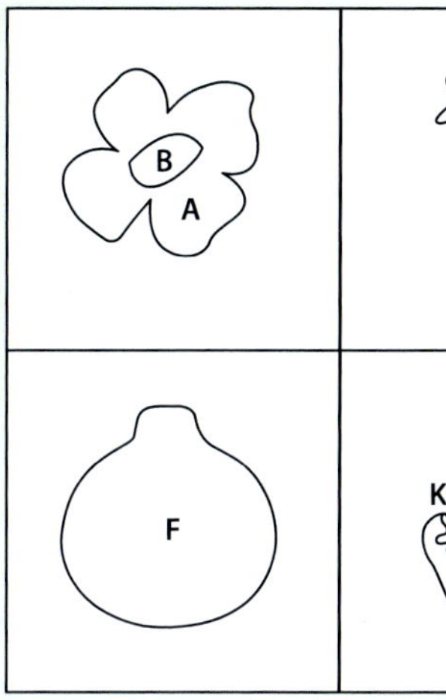

DIRECTORY BLOCK

WHAT YOU'LL NEED

- ☐ 8¹/₂" x 11" sheet of white cotton colorfast printable fabric

ASSEMBLY

1. I have provided an editable file at https://bit.ly/7561_Directory_Block. Open the file and add the information you desire, such as, the order of your blocks, your name, city, state, and date. Save the file.

2. Insert the sheet of printable fabric in your printer and print the file according to fabric manufacturer's instructions. Let the ink set for 10 minutes.

3. Soak the fabric in cold water for a few minutes. Remove fabric from water and lay it on a kitchen towel. Pat it with a paper towel (do not rub) to remove excess water and let it dry.

4. Trim **Block** to 8¹/₂" square.

BLOCK

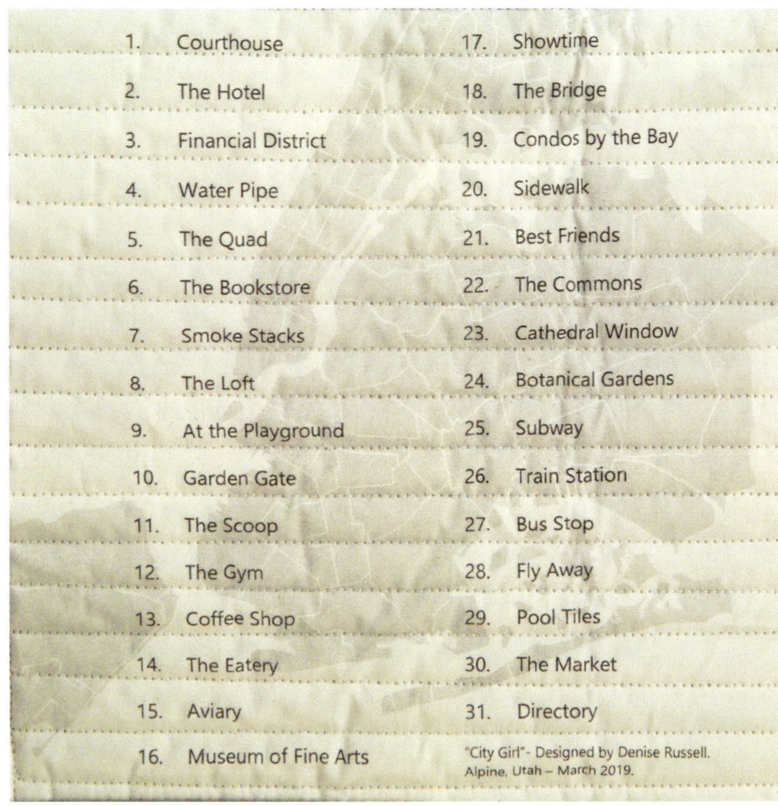

ALTERNATE BLOCKS & SASHINGS

BLOCK ASSEMBLY

*Follow **Machine Piecing**, page 86, and **Pressing**, page 87, to make block. Use a 1/4" seam allowance throughout.*

***Note:** All blocks are sprayed starched with light starch before they are stitched together into rows.*

1. Sew a 2 1/2" dark gray strip to a 2 1/2" light gray print strip to make a strip set. Do not press open. Repeat to make a total of 4 strip sets. Cut strip sets into 2 1/2" sections to make **Unit 1**. Make a total of 64 Unit 1's. Press open.

2. Sew 2 Unit 1's together to make a **4-Patch Unit**. Make 32 4-Patch Units.

3. Sew two 2 1/2" x 4 1/2" rectangles to opposite sides of one 4-Patch Unit to make **Unit 2**. Press the seam allowances away from the center. Repeat to make 32 Unit 2's.

Unit 1

4-Patch Unit

Unit 2

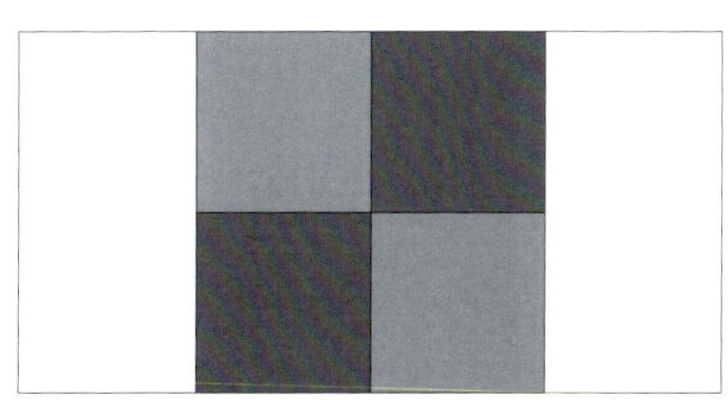

4. Sew a $4^{1}/_{2}$" white strip in between one $2^{1}/_{2}$" dark gray strip and one $2^{1}/_{2}$" light gray print strip to make a strip set. Press seam allowances to center. Repeat to make a total of 4 strip sets. Cut strip sets into $2^{1}/_{2}$" sections to make Unit 3. Make a total of 64 Unit 3's. Press open.

Unit 3

5. Noting fabric orientation, sew a Unit 3 to the top and bottom of the Unit 2's to make **Block**. Press the seam allowances in one direction.

ALTERNATE BLOCK

HORIZONTAL SASHING ASSEMBLY

1. Refer to the quilt photo for fabric placement and alternately sew seven $2^{1}/_{2}$" x $8^{1}/_{2}$" light gray/white dots sashings, three $2^{1}/_{2}$" dark gray squares and three $2^{1}/_{2}$" light gray squares together. Repeat to make a total of eight sashings. Press the seam allowances away from squares.

ASSEMBLING THE QUILT

1. Referring to the quilt photo for block placement and color orientation, lay out seven blocks and the $2^{1}/_{2}$" x $8^{1}/_{2}$" sashings in nine rows, and join the blocks and sashings together in each row. Press the seam allowances toward the sashing.

2. Insert the horizontal sashings in between the block rows, making sure to alternate the direction of sashings.

3. Matching adjacent seams, sew block rows and horizontal sashings together. Press seam allowances in one direction.

FINISHING THE QUILT

1. Follow **Quilting**, page 89, to mark, layer, and quilt as desired. Our quilt is quilted with an all-over meandering pattern.

2. Refer to **Making A Hanging Sleeve**, page 91, to make and attach a hanging sleeve, if desired.

3. Sew binding strips together end to end; press seam allowances open. Follow **Binding**, page 91, to bind quilt.

HOOP TRIO

Finished Hoop Sizes: 7" (18 cm) diameter and 9" diameter (23 cm)

SHOPPING LIST

Yardage is based on 43"/44" (109 cm/112 cm) wide fabric with a usable width of 40" (102 cm). If you use a different word, you may need a different amount of fabric for your hoop.

- ☐ 1/4 yd (23 cm) of black solid fabric for appliqués
- ☐ 1/8 yd (11 cm) of gray print fabric for appliqués
- ☐ 2 1/2" x 7" (6 cm x 18 cm) piece of orange print fabric for appliqué
- ☐ 3/8 yd (34 cm) of teal solid fabric
- ☐ 1/8 yd (11 cm) of teal print fabric
- ☐ 1/4 yd (23 cm) of yellow solid fabric
- ☐ 2 7/8" x 2 7/8" (7 cm x 7 cm) square of 15 assorted fabrics

You will also need:

- ☐ 9" (23 cm) diameter wooden embroidery hoop
- ☐ two 7" (18 cm) diameter wooden embroidery hoops
- ☐ 12" x 32" (30 cm x 81 cm) piece of batting
- ☐ paper-backed fusible web
- ☐ coordinating thread for piecing
- ☐ matching threads for machine appliqué
- ☐ tracing paper
- ☐ heavy duty thread or embroidery floss

CUTTING THE PIECES

*Follow **Rotary Cutting**, page 86, to cut fabric. Cut all strips from the selvage-to-selvage width of the fabric. All measurements include 1/4" seam allowances.*

From teal print fabric:

- Cut 1 strip 4 1/2" x fabric width. From this strip, cut 2 rectangles 4 1/2" x 11".

From yellow solid fabric:

- Cut 2 strips 2 7/8" x fabric width. From these strips, cut 15 squares 2 7/8" x 2 7/8".

From teal solid fabric:

- Cut 1 strip 9 1/4" x fabric width. From this strip, cut 1 large rectangle 9 1/4" x 13" and 2 small rectangles 6 1/2" x 11".

ASSEMBLY

*Follow **Machine Piecing**, page 86, and **Pressing**, page 87, to make projects. Use a 1/4" seam allowance throughout.*

Large Hoop Background

1. Draw a diagonal line on the wrong side of the yellow solid squares. With right sides together, place a yellow solid square on top of an assorted print square. Stitch 1/4" on each side of drawn line **(Fig. 1)**. Cut along drawn line and press toward darker fabric. Trim the dog ears to make a **Half-Square Triangle**. Trim Half-Square Triangle to 1 3/4" x 1 3/4" . Repeat with remaining yellow solid and assorted print squares to make a total of 30 Half-Square Triangles.

2. Sew 10 half-square triangles together to make **Row**. Make a total of 3 Rows. Alternating direction of each row, press seam allowances to one side. Sew rows together and press the seams open to make **Unit 1**.

3. Sew large rectangle and Unit 1 together to make large hoop background.

Small Hoop Background

1. Sew teal solid small rectangle and teal print rectangle together to make small hoop background.

Adding the Appliqués

1. Follow **Preparing Fusible Appliqués**, page 88, and use word pattern, page 95, and desired bird patterns from Aviary block, page 34, to cut word appliqué from orange print fabric and bird appliqués from black solid and gray print fabrics.

2. Position the appliqués on the background and fuse them according to the fusible web manufacturer's instructions.

3. Follow **Blanket Stitch Appliqué**, page 88, to appliqué pieces in place using matching thread.

Quilting

1. Cut one 12" square and two 10" squares from batting.

2. Center the corresponding background over each batting square. Quilt as desired. Our hoops are quilted around the word, around the birds, and in the ditch of each half-square triangle.

Finishing the Hoop

1. Center the inner hoop on top of the background. Trim the background to about 2" beyond the outer hoop edge.

2. Center the background over the inner hoop. Place the outer hoop over the background and inner hoop and tighten the turn screw. Gently pull the background evenly around the edges until the background is tight in the hoop.

3. Using heavy duty thread or embroidery floss, work Running Stitches about 1/2" from the cut edge; do not trim the floss ends. Pull the floss ends to gather the background. Tightly knot the floss ends together and trim any excess.

Fig. 1

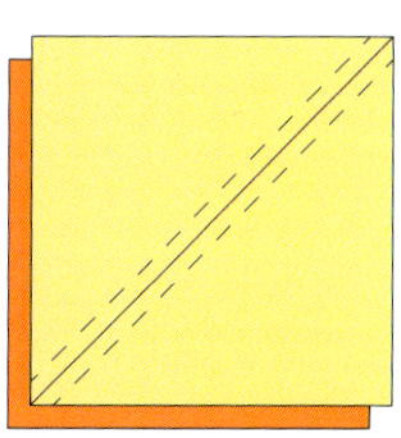

Half-Square Triangle (make 30)

Row (make 3)

Unit 1

HUGS AND HISSES PILLOW

Finished Pillow Size: 20" x 20" (51 cm x 51 cm)

SHOPPING LIST

Yardage is based on 43"/44" (109 cm/112 cm) wide fabric with a usable width of 40" (102 cm). If you use different words, you may need a different amount of fabric for your pillow.

- ☐ $6^1/_2$" x $6^1/_2$" (17 cm x 17 cm) square of blue print fabric
- ☐ $^3/_8$ yd (34 cm) of rose print fabric
- ☐ $^5/_8$ yd (57 cm) of gray print fabric
- ☐ $^1/_8$ yd (11 cm) of black/white print fabric
- ☐ $^1/_8$ yd (11 cm) of teal print fabric
- ☐ $4^1/_2$" x $6^1/_2$" (11 cm x 17 cm) rectangle of black solid fabric for appliqués
- ☐ $2^1/_2$" x 20" (6 cm x 51 cm) strip of white print fabric for appliqués

You will also need:

- ☐ 22" x 22" (59 cm x 59 cm) piece of batting
- ☐ 20" x 20" (51 cm x 51 cm) pillow form
- ☐ paper-backed fusible web
- ☐ coordinating thread for piecing
- ☐ matching threads for machine appliqué
- ☐ rose embroidery floss
- ☐ embroidery needle

CUTTING THE PIECES

*Follow **Rotary Cutting**, page 86, to cut fabric. Cut all strips from the selvage-to-selvage width of the fabric. All measurements include $^{1}/_{4}$" seam allowances.*

From rose print fabric:

- Cut 2 strips (A)$1^{1}/_{2}$" x $6^{1}/_{2}$".
- Cut 2 strips (B) $1^{1}/_{2}$" x $8^{1}/_{2}$".
- Cut 3 binding strips $2^{1}/_{2}$" x width of fabric.

From gray print fabric:

- Cut 1 strip 13" x fabric width. From this strip, cut 2 pillow backs 13" x 20".
- Cut 2 strips $4^{1}/_{8}$" x fabric width. From these strips, cut 2 top/bottom borders $4^{1}/_{8}$" x $19^{3}/_{4}$" and 2 side borders $4^{1}/_{8}$" x $12^{1}/_{2}$".
- Cut 1 strip $2^{1}/_{2}$" x fabric width. From this strip, cut 4 squares $2^{1}/_{2}$" x $2^{1}/_{2}$".

From black/white print fabric:

- Cut 1 strip $2^{1}/_{2}$" x fabric width. From this strip, cut 2 small rectangles $2^{1}/_{2}$" x $3^{1}/_{2}$" and 2 large rectangles $2^{1}/_{2}$" x $5^{1}/_{2}$".

From teal print fabric:

- Cut 1 strip $2^{1}/_{2}$" x fabric width. From this strip, cut 2 small rectangles $2^{1}/_{2}$" x $3^{1}/_{2}$" and 2 large rectangles $2^{1}/_{2}$" x $5^{1}/_{2}$".

MAKING THE PILLOW

MAKING THE PILLOW TOP

*Follow **Machine Piecing**, page 86, and **Pressing**, page 87, to make pillow. Use a $^{1}/_{4}$" seam allowance throughout.*

1. Refer to **Best Friends**, page 48, to make block, using blue square, rose print strips (A & B), and black square for appliqués.
2. Sew one gray print square in between one teal small rectangle and one black/white small rectangle to make side sashing. Make a total of 2 side sashings. Press seam allowances in one direction.

Side Sashing (make 2)

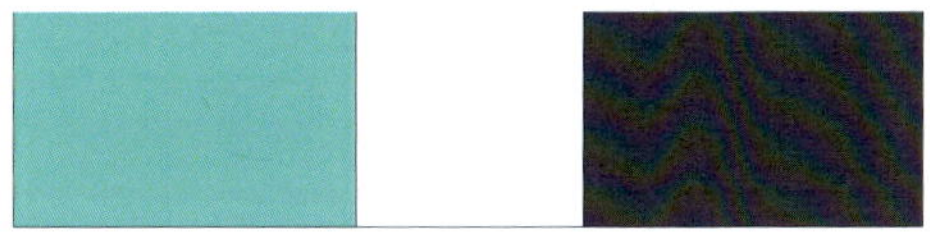

3. Noting fabric orientation, sew side sashings to opposite sides of the block. Press the seam allowances toward the block.
4. Sew a gray print square in between one teal large rectangle and one black/white large rectangle to make top sashing. Repeat to make bottom sashing. Press the seam allowances in one direction.

Top/Bottom Sashing (make 2)

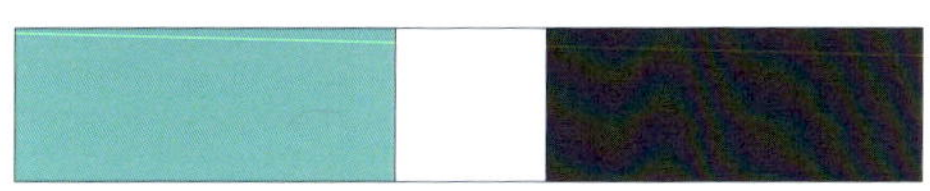

5. Noting fabric orientation, sew top sashing to top of block. Sew bottom sashing to bottom of block. Press the seam allowances toward the block.
6. Sew side borders to opposite side of block. Press the seam allowances toward the block.
7. Sew top and bottom borders to top and bottom of block. Press the top/bottom borders toward the block.

ADDING THE APPLIQUÉS

1. Follow **Preparing Fusible Appliqués**, page 88, and use patterns, page 96, to cut appliqués from white print fabric.
2. Position the letter appliqués on the pillow top and fuse them according to the fusible web manufacturer's instructions.
3. Follow **Blanket Stitch Appliqué**, page 88, to appliqué pieces in place using matching thread.
4. Using a backstitch and 3 strands of floss, embroider around desired letters very close to the appliqué stitches to ensure the letters stand out.

QUILTING

1. Place the pillow top on the batting. Follow **Quilting**, page 89, to mark, layer, and quilt as desired. Our pillow is channel quilted in the borders. Trim batting even with pillow top edges.

MAKING THE PILLOW

1. Press one long edge of each pillow back $^{1}/_{2}$" to wrong side; press to $^{1}/_{2}$" again and topstitch $^{1}/_{4}$" from the folded edge.
2. Matching **wrong** sides and raw edges, pin pillow backs on pillow top. Sew $^{1}/_{4}$" from raw edges.
3. Sew binding strips together end to end; press seam allowances open. Follow **Binding**, page 91, to bind pillow.

MARKET TOTE

Finished Size: 13"w x 4"d x 11" h
(33 cm x 10 cm x 28 cm)

SHOPPING LIST

Yardage is based on 43"/44" (109 cm/112 cm) wide fabric with a usable width of 40" (102 cm). If you use a different word, you may need a different amount of fabric for your hoop.

- ☐ 14" x 18" (36 cm x 46 cm) piece of large check fabric for tote back
- ☐ 10" x 18" (25 cm x 46 cm) piece of black and gray stripe fabric for tote front
- ☐ 4 1/2" x 18" (11 cm x 46 cm) piece of white solid fabric for tote front
- ☐ 5/8 yd (57 cm) of white/gray dot print fabric for lining
- ☐ scraps of pink, teal, and yellow print fabrics for appliqués

You will also need:

- ☐ 1/2 yd (46 cm) of heavy fusible interfacing (I used Annie's™ Soft and Stable™)
- ☐ 42" (107 cm) of black canvas strap
- ☐ paper-backed fusible web
- ☐ coordinating thread for piecing
- ☐ matching threads for machine appliqué

CUTTING THE PIECES

*Follow **Rotary Cutting**, page 86, to cut fabric. Cut all strips from the selvage-to-selvage width of the fabric. All measurements include 1/4" seam allowances.*

From white/gray dot print fabric for lining:

- Cut 2 lining rectangles 14" x 18".

From fusible interfacing:

- Cut 2 rectangles 14" x 18".

ASSEMBLY

*Follow **Machine Piecing**, page 86, and **Pressing**, page 87, to make projects. Use a 1/2" seam allowance unless otherwise stated.*

TOTE FRONT

1. Sew white solid rectangle to gray stripe rectangle along long edges. Press the seam allowances toward the strip fabric.

ADDING THE APPLIQUÉS

1. Follow **Preparing Fusible Appliqués**, page 88, and use patterns from **The Market** block, page 66, to cut appliqués from scrap fabrics.
2. Position the appliqués on the white rectangle and fuse them according to the fusible web manufacturer's instructions.
3. Follow **Blanket Stitch Appliqué**, page 88, to appliqué pieces in place using matching thread.

ASSEMBLING THE TOTE

1. Follow manufacturer's instructions to fuse one interfacing to the tote front and tote back.
2. Refer to **Fig. 1** to cut a 2" notch from the bottom corners of the tote front and tote back **(Fig. 1)**.

Fig. 1

3. Quilt the tote front and tote back as desired. We quilted evenly spaced horizontal lines on the front and vertical and horizontal lines with the lines of the check on the back.
4. Matching right sides, sew the tote front and tote back together along the sides and bottom.
5. To box bottom, match right sides and align side seam with bottom seam; sew across ends **(Fig. 2)**

Fig. 2

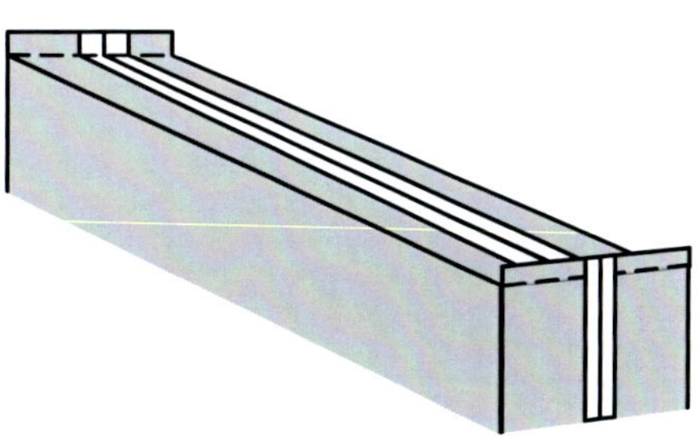

6. Repeat Steps 2 and 4-5 using lining rectangles, leaving a 4" opening in bottom seam.
7. For handles, cut canvas strap into two pieces. Pin raw edges of one handle even with the top edge and 6" from side seams **(Fig. 3)**; baste in place. Repeat for remaining handle on tote back.

Fig. 3

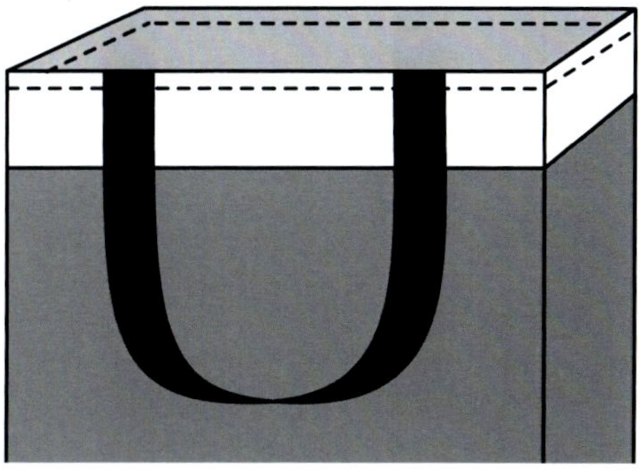

8. Turn the lining right side out and place it inside the outer tote so right sides are facing and handles are sandwiched between layers. Matching side seams, pin the top edge of the tote and lining together. Beginning at side seam, sew around the top of the tote.
9. Turn the tote right side out through the opening in the lining; press. Fold the edges of the lining opening 1/2" to wrong side and press. Sew the opening closed.
10. Topstitch about 1/8" from the top edge of the tote.

METRO TABLE RUNNER

Finished Wall Hanging Size:
18½" x 52½" (47 cm x 133 cm)

SHOPPING LIST

Yardage is based on 43"/44" (109 cm/112 cm) wide fabric with a usable width of 40" (102 cm).

- ☐ 3/8 yd (34 cm) of dark gray print fabric (includes binding)
- ☐ 1/4 yd (23 cm) of light gray print fabric
- ☐ 3/4 yd (69 cm) of white solid fabric
- ☐ 1/4 yd (23 cm) of purple print fabric
- ☐ 1/4 yd (23 cm) of fuchsia print fabric for binding
- ☐ 1 3/8 yds (1.3 m) of fabric for backing
- ☐ 1/4 yd (23 cm) of fuchsia print fabric for binding

You will also need:

- ☐ 22" x 56" (56 cm x 142 cm) piece of batting
- ☐ coordinating thread for piecing

CUTTING THE PIECES

*Follow **Rotary Cutting**, page 86, to cut fabric. Cut all strips from the selvage-to-selvage width of the fabric. All measurements include $^{1}/_{4}$" seam allowances.*

From dark gray print fabric:

- Cut 2 strips $1^{1}/_{2}$" wide. From these strips, cut 12 rectangles $1^{1}/_{2}$" x $3^{1}/_{2}$".
- Cut 3 strips $1^{1}/_{2}$" wide. From these strips, cut 36 rectangles $1^{1}/_{2}$" x $2^{1}/_{2}$".
- Cut 3 binding strips $2^{1}/_{2}$" wide.

From light gray print fabric:

- Cut 2 strips $1^{1}/_{2}$" wide. From these strips, cut 12 rectangles $1^{1}/_{2}$" x $3^{1}/_{2}$".
- Cut 2 strips $1^{1}/_{2}$" wide. From these strips, cut 18 rectangles $1^{1}/_{2}$" x $2^{1}/_{2}$".

From white solid fabric:

- Cut 3 strips $2^{1}/_{2}$" wide. From these strips, cut 48 squares $2^{1}/_{2}$" x $2^{1}/_{2}$".
- Cut 1 strip $1^{1}/_{2}$" wide. From this strip, cut 6 rectangles $1^{1}/_{2}$" x $2^{1}/_{2}$".
- Cut 7 strips $2^{1}/_{2}$" wide.

From purple print fabric:

- Cut 3 strips $1^{1}/_{2}$" wide.

MAKING THE TABLE RUNNER TOP

*Follow **Machine Piecing**, page 86, and **Pressing**, page 87, to make wall hanging. Use a $^{1}/_{4}$" seam allowance throughout.*

1. Follow **Subway** block, page 56, to make 6 blocks using dark gray print rectangles, light gray print rectangles, and white solid rectangles and squares.
2. Noting block orientation, sew the blocks together and press the seam allowances in one direction.
3. Sew the $2^{1}/_{2}$" wide white solid strips together end to end using diagonal seams **(Fig. 1)**. Cut four $48^{1}/_{2}$" long borders and two $18^{1}/_{2}$" short borders. Set two long borders and short borders aside.

Fig 1

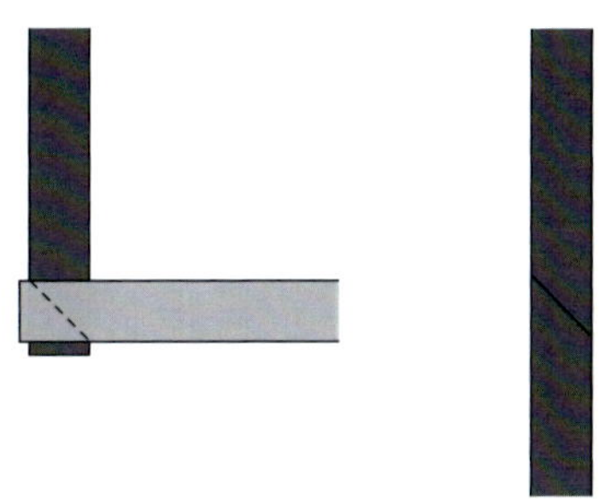

4. Sew one border to each long edge of the table runner top.
5. Repeat Steps 3-4 using purple print strips to make two $48^{1}/_{2}$" borders and sew to each long edge of the table runner top.
6. Sew remaining white borders to each long edge of the table runner top.
7. Sew one short border to each short edge of table runner.

FINISHING THE TABLE RUNNER

1. Follow **Quilting**, page 89, to mark, layer, and quilt as desired. Our quilt is channel quilted with diagonal lines.
2. Sew binding strips together end to end; press seam allowances open. Follow **Binding**, page 91, to bind quilt.

POPCORN WALL HANGING

Finished Wall Hanging Size:
15$^{1}/_{2}$" x 22$^{1}/_{2}$" (39 cm x 57 cm)

SHOPPING LIST

Yardage is based on 43"/44" (109 cm/112 cm) wide fabric with a usable width of 40" (102 cm). If you use different words, you may need a different amount of fabric for your wall hanging.

- ☐ 16$^{1}/_{2}$" x 23$^{1}/_{2}$" (42 cm x 60 cm) rectangle of black print fabric for background
- ☐ 16$^{1}/_{2}$" x 23$^{1}/_{2}$" (42 cm x 60 cm) rectangle of black solid fabric for backing
- ☐ 5" x 5" (13 cm x 13 cm) square of red check fabric for appliqué
- ☐ 7" x 9" (18 cm x 23 cm) rectangle of white print fabric for appliqués
- ☐ 2$^{1}/_{2}$" x 40" (6 cm x 102 cm) strip of teal print fabric for appliqués
- ☐ 2$^{1}/_{2}$" x 9" (6 cm x 23 cm) strip of yellow print fabric for appliqués
- ☐ 2 strips 2$^{1}/_{2}$" x 40" (6 cm x 102 cm) of floral print fabric for binding

You will also need:

- ☐ 16$^{1}/_{2}$" x 23$^{1}/_{2}$" (42 cm x 60 cm) piece of batting
- ☐ paper-backed fusible web
- ☐ coordinating thread for piecing
- ☐ matching threads for machine appliqué

MAKING THE WALL HANGING TOP

*Follow **Machine Piecing**, page 86, and **Pressing**, page 87, to make wall hanging. Use a 1/4" seam allowance throughout.*

1. Follow **Preparing Fusible Appliqués**, page 88, and use word pattern, pages 94-95, and popcorn and box patterns from **Show Time** block, page 40, to cut word appliqué from teal and yellow print fabrics, popcorn appliqués from white print fabric, and popcorn box appliqué from red check fabric.

2. Position the appliqués on the background and fuse them according to the fusible web manufacturer's instructions.

3. Follow **Blanket Stitch Appliqué**, page 88, to appliqué pieces in place using matching thread.

FINISHING THE QUILT

1. Follow **Quilting**, page 89, to mark, layer, and quilt as desired. Our quilt is quilted around each appliqué and with a meandering stitch over the background.

2. Trim the wall hanging to 15 1/2" x 22 1/2".

3. Refer to **Making A Hanging Sleeve**, page 91, to make and attach a hanging sleeve, if desired.

4. Sew binding strips together end to end; press seam allowances open. Follow **Binding**, page 91, to bind quilt.

UPS & DOWNS WALLHANGING

Finished Wall Hanging Size:
18" x 22" (46 cm x 56 cm)

SHOPPING LIST

Yardage is based on 43"/44" (109 cm/112 cm) wide fabric with a usable width of 40" (102 cm).

- ☐ 5 1/2" x 18" (14 cm x 46 cm) strip of black/blue plaid fabric
- ☐ 4" x 18" (10 cm x 46 cm) rectangle of light green print fabric
- ☐ 1/4 yd (23 cm) of turquoise print fabric
- ☐ 1/4 yd (23 cm) of off-white print fabric
- ☐ 1 1/2" x 40" (3 cm x 102 cm) strip of dark green solid fabric
- ☐ 7 1/2" x 7 1/2" (19 cm x 19 cm) square of black solid fabric for appliqués
- ☐ 2 1/2" x 9" (6 cm x 23 cm) rectangle of purple print fabric for appliqués
- ☐ 2 1/2" x 18" (6 cm x 46 cm) strip of pink print fabric for appliqués
- ☐ 22" x 26" (56 cm x 66 cm) piece of fabric for backing
- ☐ 1/4 yd (23 cm) of fuchsia print fabric for binding

You will also need:

- ☐ 22" x 26" (56 cm x 66 cm) piece of batting
- ☐ paper-backed fusible web
- ☐ coordinating thread for piecing
- ☐ matching threads for machine appliqué

CUTTING THE PIECES

*Follow **Rotary Cutting**, page 86, to cut fabric. Cut all strips from the selvage-to-selvage width of the fabric. All measurements include $\frac{1}{4}$" seam allowances.*

From turquoise print fabric:

- Cut 2 strips $3\frac{7}{8}$" x fabric width. From these strips, cut 12 squares $3\frac{7}{8}$" x $3\frac{7}{8}$".

From off-white solid fabric:

- Cut 2 strips $3\frac{7}{8}$" x fabric width. From these strips, cut 12 squares $3\frac{7}{8}$" x $3\frac{7}{8}$".

From dark green solid fabric:

- Cut 2 strips $1\frac{1}{2}$" x 18".

From fuchsia print fabric:

- Cut 3 binding strips $2\frac{1}{2}$" x fabric width.

MAKING THE WALL HANGING TOP

*Follow **Machine Piecing**, page 86, and **Pressing**, page 87, to make wall hanging. Use a $\frac{1}{4}$" seam allowance throughout.*

1. Draw a diagonal line on the wrong side of the off-white solid squares. With right sides together, place a off-white solid square on top of a turquoise print square. Stitch $\frac{1}{4}$" on each side of drawn line (**Fig. 1**). Cut along drawn line and press toward darker fabric. Trim the dog ears to make a **Half-Square Triangle**. Repeat with remaining off white and turquoise squares to make a total of 24 half-square triangles.

2. Sew 6 half-square triangles together to make **Row A**. Press the seam allowances in one direction. Make 2 Row A's.

3. Sew 6 half-square triangles together to make **Row B**. Press the seam allowances in one direction. Make 2 Row B's.

4. Sew 1 Row A and 1 Row B together to make **Unit 1**. Make 2 Unit 1's.

5. Sew together the blue/black plaid rectangle and light green rectangle to make quilt center. Press the seam allowances toward the dark fabric.

6. Sew one $1\frac{1}{2}$" x 18" lime strip to the top and bottom of the quilt center. Press the seam allowances toward the lime strips.

7. Noting orientation, sew Unit 1's to top and bottom of quilt. Press the seams toward the lime strip.

Fig. 1

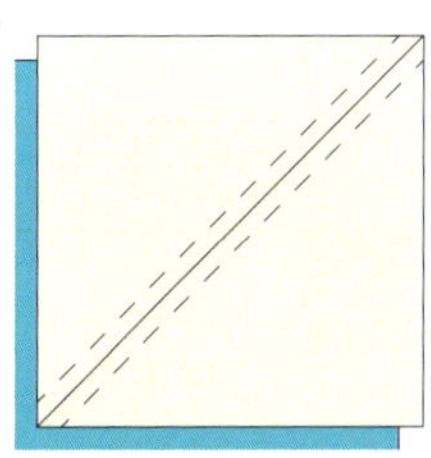

Half-Square Triangle
(make 24)

Row A (make 2)

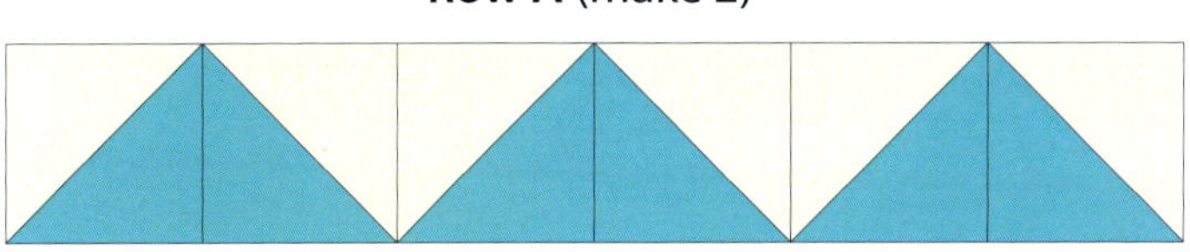

Row B (make 2)

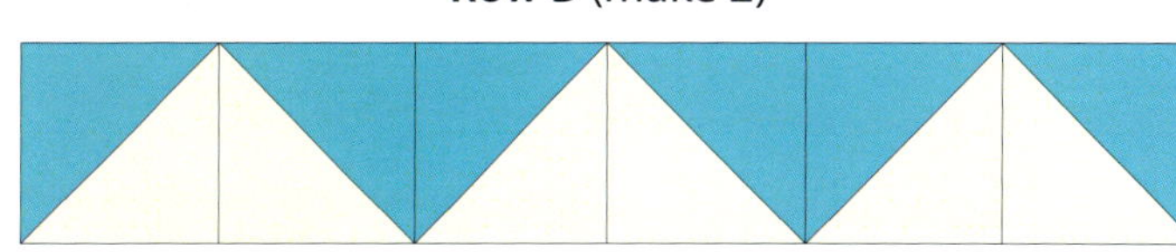

Unit 1 (make 2)

ADDING THE APPLIQUÉS

1. Follow **Preparing Fusible Appliqués**, page 88, and use word pattern, page 94, and appliqué patterns from **The Gym** block, page 28, to cut word appliqué from purple and pink print fabrics and body builder appliqués from black solid fabric.

2. Position the appliqués on the background and fuse them according to the fusible web manufacturer's instructions.

3. Follow **Blanket Stitch Appliqué**, page 88, to appliqué pieces in place using matching thread.

FINISHING THE QUILT

1. Follow **Quilting**, page 89, to mark, layer, and quilt as desired. Our quilt is quilted around each appliqué and with a meandering stitch over the background.

2. Trim the wall hanging to 18" x 22".

3. Refer to **Making A Hanging Sleeve**, page 91, to make and attach a hanging sleeve, if desired.

4. Sew binding strips together end to end; press seam allowances open. Follow **Binding**, page 91, to bind quilt.

GENERAL INSTRUCTIONS

To make your quilting easier and more enjoyable, we encourage you to carefully read all of the general instructions, study the color photographs, and familiarize yourself with the individual project instructions before beginning a project.

FABRICS

SELECTING FABRICS

Choose high-quality, medium-weight 100% cotton fabrics. All-cotton fabrics hold a crease better, fray less, and are easier to quilt than cotton/polyester blends.

Yardage requirements listed for each project are based on 43"/44" wide fabric with a "usable" width of 40" after shrinkage and trimming selvages. Actual usable width will probably vary slightly from fabric to fabric. Our recommended yardage lengths should be adequate for occasional re-squaring of fabric when many cuts are required.

PREPARING FABRICS

This quilt uses many small pieces of fabric and is perfect for using your stash and scraps. Pre-washng small fabric pieces may cause edges to ravel. As a result, your small pieces may not be large enough to cut all of the pieces required for your project. Therefore, we do not recommend pre-washing any of your fabrics.

Before cutting, prepare fabrics with a steam iron set on cotton and starch or sizing. The starch or sizing will give the fabric a crisp finish. This will make cutting more accurate and may make piecing easier.

ROTARY CUTTING

- Place fabric on work surface with fold closest to you.
- Cut all strips from the selvage-to-selvage width of the fabric unless otherwise indicated in project instructions.
- Square left edge of fabric using rotary cutter and rulers **(Figs. 1-2)**.
- To cut each strip required for a project, place ruler over cut edge of fabric, aligning desired marking on ruler with cut edge; make cut **(Fig. 3)**.
- When cutting several strips from a single piece of fabric, it is important to make sure that cuts remain at a perfect right angle to the fold; square fabric as needed.

Fig. 1

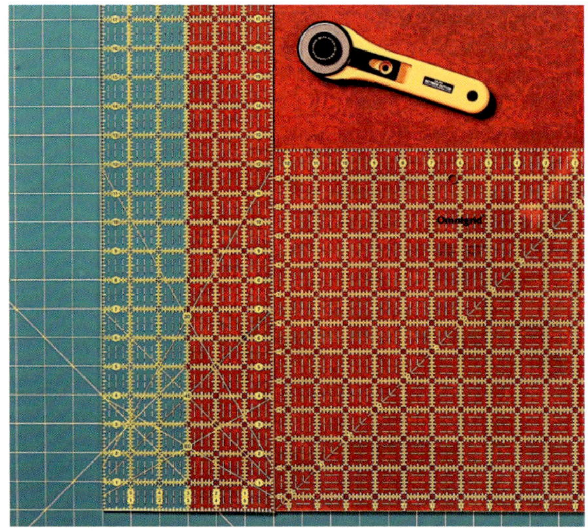

Fig. 2

Fig. 3

MACHINE PIECING

Precise cutting, followed by accurate piecing, will ensure that all pieces of quilt top fit together well.

- Set sewing machine stitch length for approximately 11 stitches per inch.
- Use neutral-colored general-purpose sewing thread (not quilting thread) in needle and in bobbin.
- An accurate 1/4" seam allowance is *essential*. Presser feet that are 1/4" wide are available for most sewing machines.
- When piecing, always place pieces right sides together and match raw edges; pin if necessary.
- Chain piecing saves time and will usually result in more accurate piecing.
- Trim away points of seam allowances that extend beyond edges of sewn pieces.

SEWING STRIP SETS

When there are several strips to assemble into a strip set, first sew strips together into pairs, then sew pairs together to form strip set. To help avoid distortion, sew seams in opposite directions **(Fig. 4)**.

Fig. 4

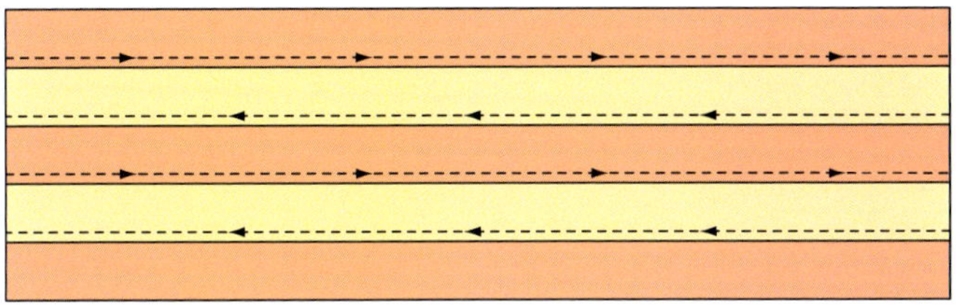

SEWING ACROSS SEAM INTERSECTIONS

When sewing across intersection of two seams, place pieces right sides together and match seams exactly, making sure seam allowances are pressed in opposite directions **(Fig. 5)**.

Fig. 5

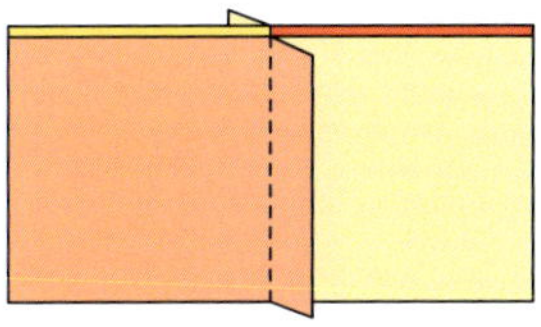

SEWING SHARP POINTS

To ensure sharp points when joining triangular or diagonal pieces, stitch across the center of the "X" (shown in pink) formed on wrong side by previous seams **(Fig. 6)**.

Fig. 6

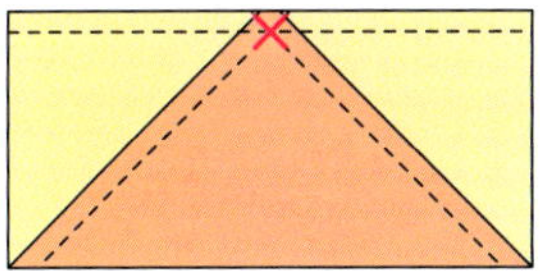

PRESSING

- Use steam iron set on "Cotton" for all pressing.
- Press after sewing each seam.
- Seam allowances are almost always pressed to one side, usually toward darker fabric. However, to reduce bulk it may occasionally be necessary to press seam allowances toward the lighter fabric or even to press them open.
- To prevent dark fabric seam allowance from showing through light fabric, trim darker seam allowance slightly narrower than lighter seam allowance.
- To press long seams, such as those in long strip sets, without curving or other distortion, lay strips across width of the ironing board.
- When sewing blocks into rows, seam allowances may be pressed in one direction in odd numbered rows and in the opposite direction in even numbered rows. When sewing rows together, press seam allowances in one direction.

MACHINE APPLIQUÉ

TIPS:

1. I prefer to use the blanket stitch on all my machine appliqué projects because it looks less dense than the satin stitch. I apply a coat of Dritz® Fray Check directly onto the stitches to prevent excessive fraying.
2. I do not use stabilizer on the back of the appliqué blocks. How do the stitches look so good? I use the same thread weight [40 wt.] and color on the top and in the bobbin.
3. When appliquéing sharp points, I switch from blanket stitch to straight stitch to ensure the fabric is secure and the stitches only cover the appliqué.

PREPARING FUSIBLE APPLIQUÉS

White or light-colored fabrics may need to be lined with fusible interfacing before applying fusible web to prevent darker fabrics from showing through.

1. Place paper-backed fusible web, paper side up, over appliqué pattern. Trace pattern onto paper side of web with pencil as many times as indicated in project instructions for a single fabric.
2. Cut each shape $^{1}/_{8}$" outside the traced line. Follow manufacturer's instructions to fuse web to the wrong side of the fabrics. Do not remove paper backing.
3. Use scissors to cut out appliqué pieces along traced lines. Remove paper backing from all pieces.

BLANKET STITCH APPLIQUÉ

These projects use a Blanket Stitch along the exposed raw edges of the appliqué pieces. Refer to your owner's manual for set-up. If your machine does not have this stitch, try any of the decorative stitches your machine has until you are satisfied with the look. A Satin Stitch can also be used. Satin Stitch is a thick, smooth, almost solid line of zigzag stitching that covers the raw edges.

1. Thread sewing machine and bobbin with 100% cotton thread in desired weight.
2. Attach an open-toe presser foot. Select far right needle position and needle down (if your machine has these features).
3. Bring bobbin thread to the top of the fabric by lowering then raising the needle, bringing up the bobbin thread loop. Pull the loop all the way to the surface.
4. Begin by stitching two or three stitches in place (drop feed dogs or set stitch length at 0), or use your machine's lock stitch feature, if equipped, to anchor thread. Return setting to selected Blanket Stitch.
5. Most of the Blanket Stitch should be on the appliqué with the right edges of the stitch falling at the very outside edge of the appliqué. Stitch over all exposed raw edges of appliqué pieces.
6. *(**Note:** Dots on **Figs. 7-11** indicate where to leave needle in fabric when pivoting.)* Always stopping with needle down in background fabric, refer to **Fig. 7** to stitch outside points like tips of leaves. Stop one stitch short of point. Raise presser foot. Pivot project slightly, lower presser foot, and make an angled Stitch 1. Take next stitch, stop at point, and pivot so Stitch 2 will be perpendicular to point. Pivot slightly to make Stitch 3. Continue stitching.

Fig. 7

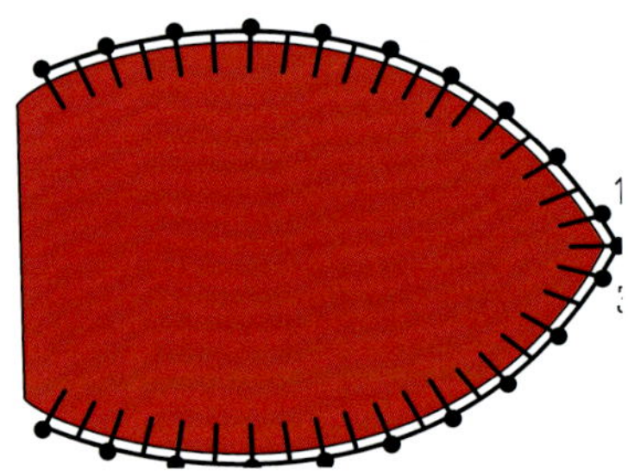

7. For outside corners **(Fig. 8)**, stitch to corner, stopping with needle in background fabric. Raise presser foot. Pivot project, lower presser foot, and take an angled stitch. Raise presser foot. Pivot project, lower presser foot and stitch adjacent side.

Fig. 8

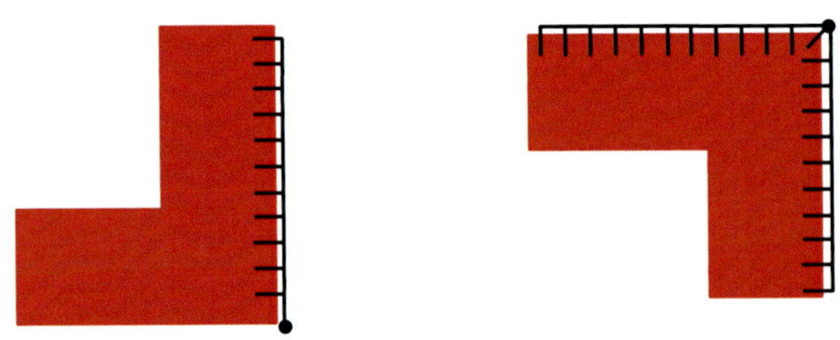

8. For inside corners **(Fig. 9)**, stitch to the corner, taking the last bite at corner and stopping with the needle down in background fabric. Raise presser foot. Pivot project, lower presser foot, and take an angled stitch. Raise presser foot. Pivot project, lower presser foot and stitch adjacent side.

Fig. 9

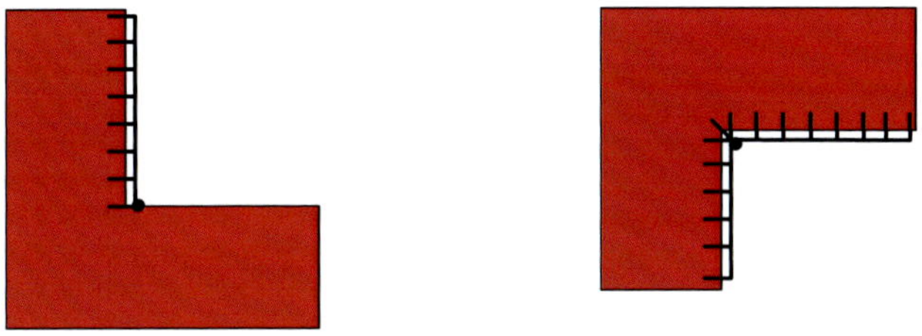

9. When stitching outside curves (**Fig. 10**), stop with needle down in background fabric. Raise presser foot and pivot project as needed. Lower presser foot and continue stitching, pivoting as often as necessary to follow curve. Small circles may require pivoting between each stitch.

Fig. 10

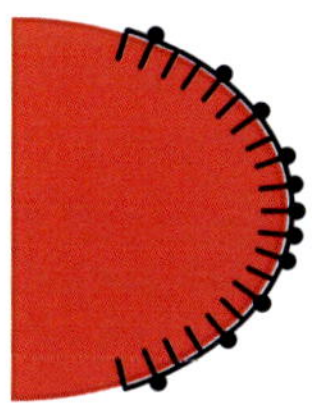

10. When stitching inside curves (**Fig. 11**), stop with needle down in background fabric. Raise presser foot and pivot project as needed. Lower presser foot and continue stitching, pivoting as often as necessary to follow curve.

Fig. 11

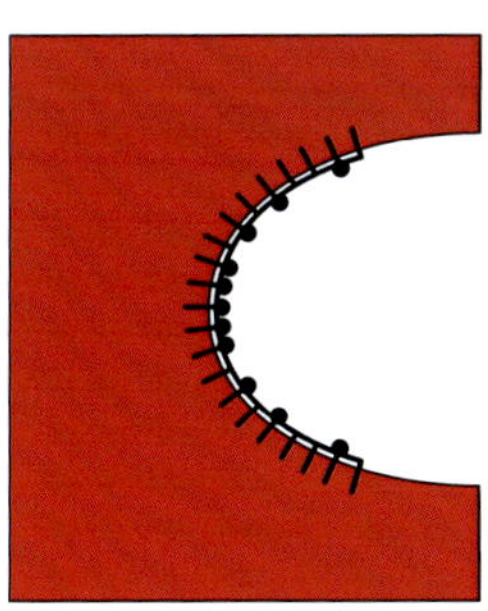

11. When stopping stitching, use a lock stitch to sew 5 or 6 stitches in place or use a needle to pull threads to wrong side of background fabric (**Fig. 12**); knot, then trim ends.

Fig. 12

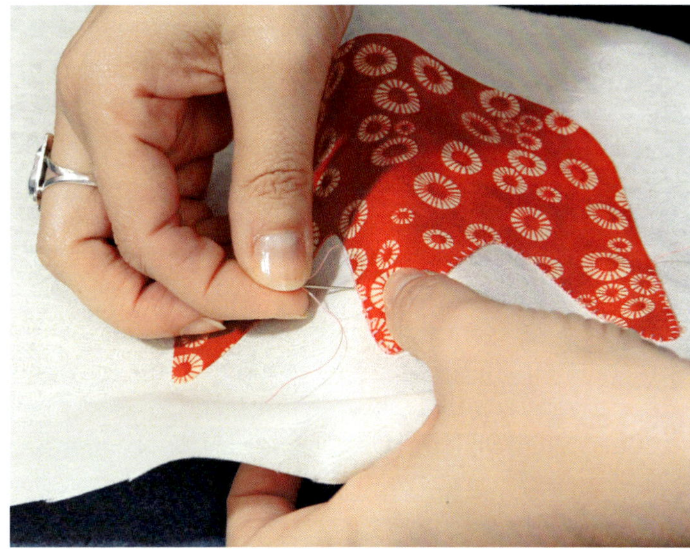

QUILTING

Quilting holds the three layers (top, batting, and backing) of the quilt together and can be done by hand or machine. Because marking, layering, and quilting are interrelated and may be done in different orders depending on circumstances, please read entire ***Quilting*** *section, pages 89-91, before beginning project.*

MARKING QUILTING LINES

Quilting lines may be marked using fabric marking pencils, chalk markers, or water- or air-soluble pens.

Simple quilting designs may be marked with chalk or chalk pencil after basting. A small area may be marked, then quilted, before moving to next area to be marked. Intricate designs should be marked before basting using a more durable marker.

Caution: Pressing may permanently set some marks. **Test** different markers **on scrap fabric** to find one that marks clearly and can be thoroughly removed.

A wide variety of pre-cut quilting stencils, as well as entire books of quilting patterns, are available. Using a stencil makes it easier to mark intricate or repetitive designs.

PREPARING THE BACKING

To allow for slight shifting of quilt top during quilting, backing should be approximately 4" larger on all sides. Yardage requirements listed for quilt backings are calculated for 43"/44"w fabric. Using 90"w or 108"w fabric for the backing of a bed-sized quilt may eliminate piecing. To piece a backing using 43"/44"w fabric, use the following instructions.

1. Measure length and width of quilt top; add 8" to each measurement.
2. Cut backing fabric into two lengths slightly longer than determined *length* measurement. Trim selvages. Place lengths with right sides facing and sew long edges together, forming tube **(Fig. 13)**. Match seams and press along one fold **(Fig. 14)**. Cut along pressed fold to form single piece **(Fig. 15)**.

Fig. 13

Fig. 14

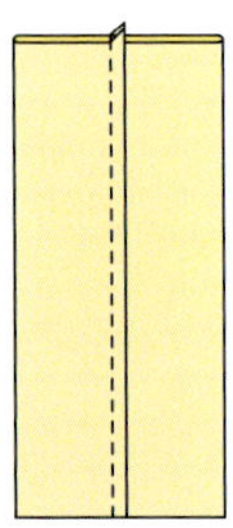

Fig. 15

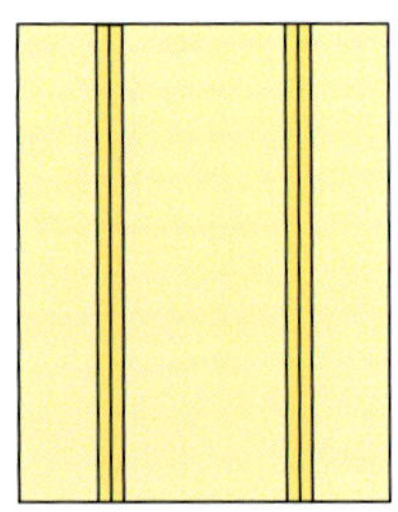

3. If determined width is more than 79", it may require less fabric yardage if the backing is pieced horizontally. Divide determined *length* measurement by 40" to determine how many widths will be needed. Cut required number of widths the determined *width* measurement. Trim selvages. Sew long edges together to form single piece.
4. Trim backing to size determined in Step 1; press seam allowances open.

CHOOSING THE BATTING

The appropriate batting will make quilting easier. For fine hand quilting, choose low-loft batting. All cotton or cotton/polyester blend battings work well for machine quilting because the cotton helps "grip" quilt layers. If quilt is to be tied, a high-loft batting, sometimes called extra-loft or fat batting, may be used to make quilt "fluffy."

Types of batting include cotton, polyester, wool, cotton/polyester blend, cotton/wool blend, and silk.

When selecting batting, refer to package labels for characteristics and care instructions. Cut batting same size as prepared backing.

ASSEMBLING THE QUILT

1. Examine wrong side of quilt top closely; trim any seam allowances and clip any threads that may show through front of the quilt. Press quilt top, being careful not to "set" any marked quilting lines.
2. Place backing *wrong* side up on flat surface. Use masking tape to tape edges of backing to surface. Place batting on top of backing fabric. Smooth batting gently, being careful not to stretch or tear. Center quilt top *right* side up on batting.
3. Use 1" rustproof safety pins to "pin-baste" all layers together, spacing pins approximately 4" apart. Begin at center and work toward outer edges to secure all layers. If possible, place pins away from areas that will be quilted, although pins may be removed as needed when quilting.

MACHINE QUILTING METHODS

Use general-purpose thread in bobbin. Do not use quilting thread. Thread the needle of machine with general-purpose thread or transparent monofilament thread to make quilting blend with quilt top fabrics. Use decorative thread, such as a metallic or contrasting-color general-purpose thread, to make quilting lines stand out more.

Straight-Line Quilting

The term "straight-line" is somewhat deceptive, since curves (especially gentle ones) as well as straight lines can be stitched with this technique.

1. Set stitch length for six to ten stitches per inch and attach walking foot to sewing machine.
2. Determine which section of quilt will have longest continuous quilting line, oftentimes area from center top to center bottom. Roll up and secure each edge of quilt to help reduce the bulk, keeping fabrics smooth. Smaller projects may not need to be rolled.
3. Begin stitching on longest quilting line, using very short stitches for the first 1/4" to "lock" quilting. Stitch across project, using one hand on each side of walking foot to slightly spread fabric and to guide fabric through machine. Lock stitches at end of quilting line.
4. Continue machine quilting, stitching longer quilting lines first to stabilize quilt before moving on to other areas.

Free-Motion Quilting

Free-motion quilting may be free form or may follow a marked pattern.

1. Attach darning foot to sewing machine and lower or cover feed dogs.
2. Position quilt under darning foot; lower foot. Holding top thread, take a stitch and pull bobbin thread to top of quilt. To "lock" beginning of quilting line, hold top and bobbin threads while making three to five stitches in place.
3. Use one hand on each side of darning foot to slightly spread fabric and to move fabric through the machine. Even stitch length is achieved by using smooth, flowing hand motion and steady machine speed. Slow machine speed and fast hand movement will create long stitches. Fast machine speed and slow hand movement will create short stitches. Move quilt sideways, back and forth, in a circular motion, or in a random motion to create desired designs; do not rotate quilt. Lock stitches at end of each quilting line.

MAKING A HANGING SLEEVE

Attaching a hanging sleeve to back of wall hanging or quilt before the binding is added allows project to be displayed on wall.

1. Measure width of quilt top edge and subtract 1". Cut piece of fabric 7"w by determined measurement.
2. Press short edges of fabric piece 1/4" to wrong side; press edges 1/4" to wrong side again and machine stitch in place.
3. Matching wrong sides, fold piece in half lengthwise to form tube.
4. Follow project instructions to sew binding to quilt top and to trim backing and batting. Before Blindstitching binding to backing, match raw edges and stitch hanging sleeve to center top edge on back of quilt.
5. Finish binding quilt, treating hanging sleeve as part of backing.
6. Blindstitch bottom of hanging sleeve to backing, taking care not to stitch through to front of quilt.

BINDING

Binding encloses the raw edges of quilt. Because of its stretchiness, bias binding works well for binding projects with curves or rounded corners and tends to lie smooth and flat in any given circumstance. Binding may also be cut from straight lengthwise or crosswise grain of fabric.

MAKING STRAIGHT-GRAIN BINDING

1. Cut lengthwise or crosswise strips of binding fabric the determined length and the width called for in project instructions. Strips may be pieced to achieve necessary length.
2. Matching wrong sides and raw edges, press strip(s) in half lengthwise to complete binding.

ATTACHING BINDING WITH MITERED CORNERS

1. Beginning with one end near center on bottom edge of quilt, lay binding around quilt to make sure that seams in binding will not end up at a corner. Adjust placement if necessary. Matching raw edges of binding to raw edge of quilt top, pin binding to right side of quilt along one edge.
2. When you reach first corner, mark 1/4" from corner of quilt top **(Fig. 16)**.

Fig. 16

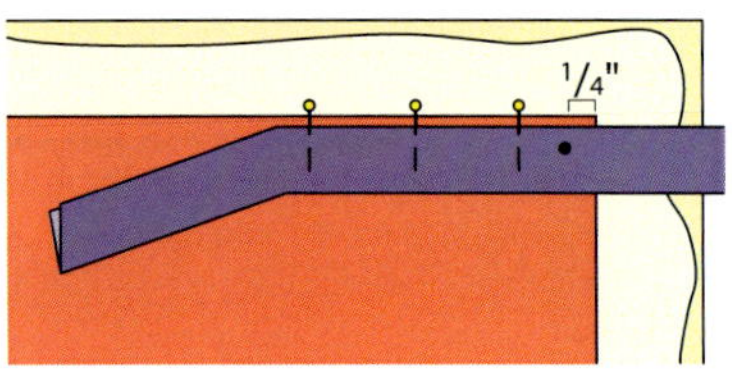

3. Beginning approximately 10" from end of binding and using 1/4" seam allowance, sew binding to quilt, backstitching at beginning of stitching and at mark **(Fig. 17)**. Lift needle out of fabric and clip thread.

Fig. 17

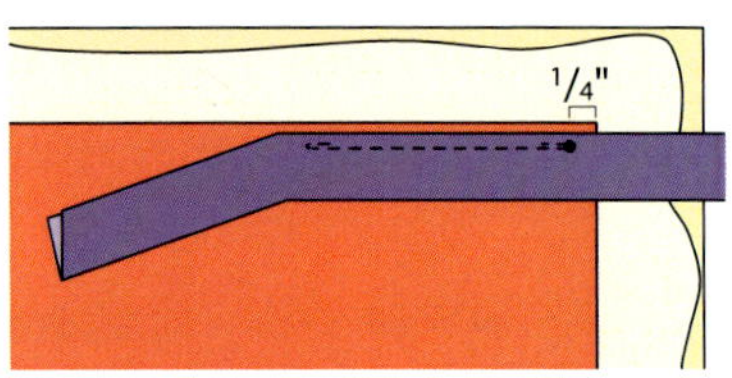

4. Fold binding as shown in **Figs. 18-19** and pin binding to adjacent side, matching raw edges. When you've reached the next corner, mark 1/4" from edge of quilt top.

Fig. 18

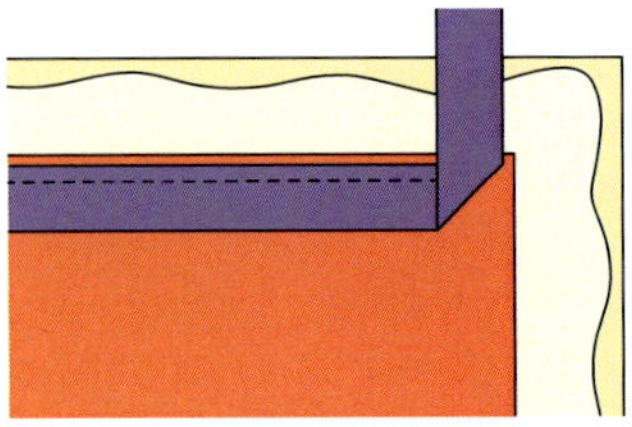

Fig. 19

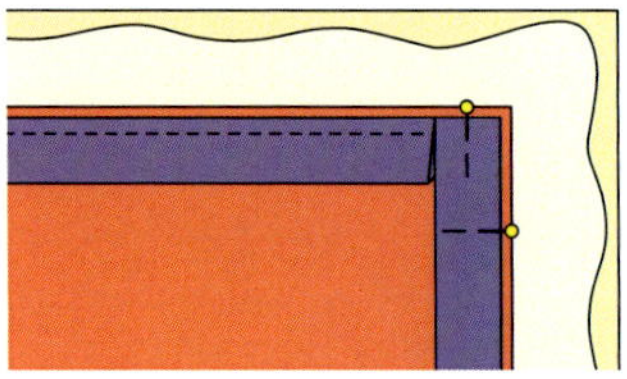

5. Backstitching at edge of quilt top, sew pinned binding to quilt **(Fig. 20)**; backstitch at the next mark. Lift needle out of fabric and clip thread.

Fig. 20

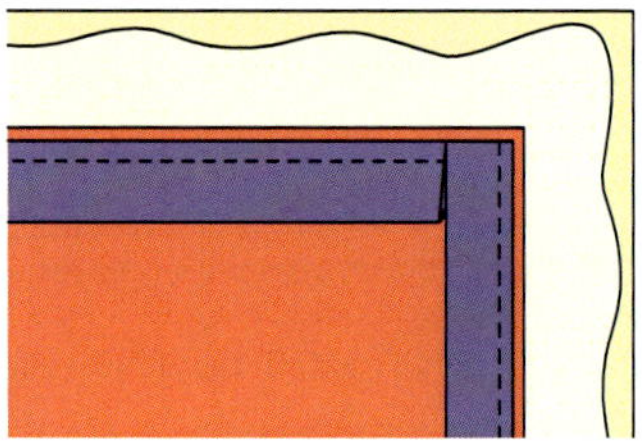

6. Continue sewing binding to quilt, stopping approximately 10" from starting point **(Fig. 21)**.

Fig. 21

7. Bring beginning and end of binding to center of opening and fold each end back, leaving a 1/4" space between folds **(Fig. 22)**. Finger press folds.

Fig. 22

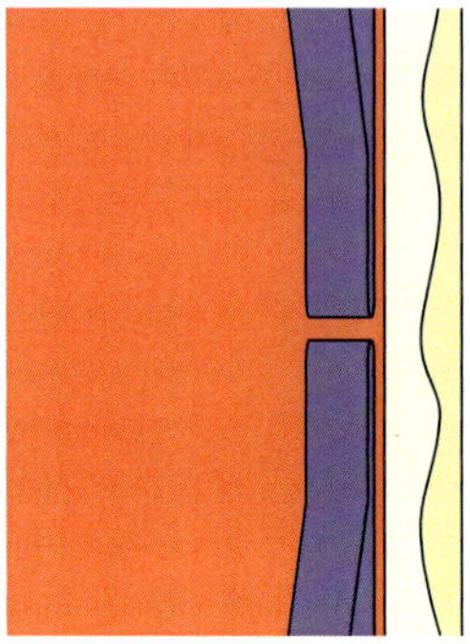

8. Unfold ends of binding and draw a line across wrong side in finger-pressed crease. Draw a line through the lengthwise pressed fold of binding at the same spot to create a cross mark. With edge of ruler at cross mark, line up 45° angle marking on ruler with one long side of binding. Draw a diagonal line from edge to edge. Repeat on remaining end, making sure that the two diagonal lines are angled the same way **(Fig. 23)**.

Fig. 23

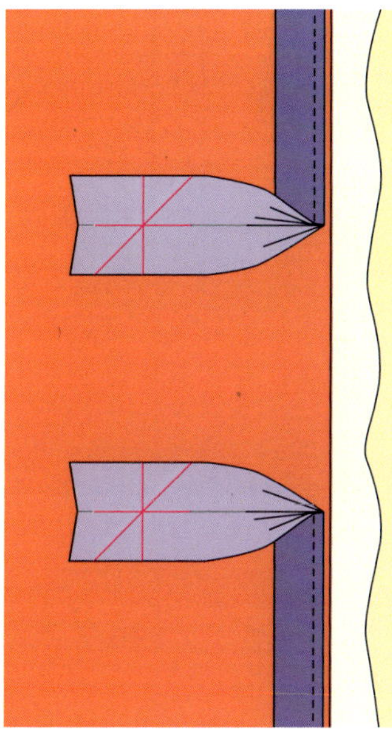

9. Matching right sides and diagonal lines, pin binding ends together at right angles **(Fig. 24)**.

Fig. 24

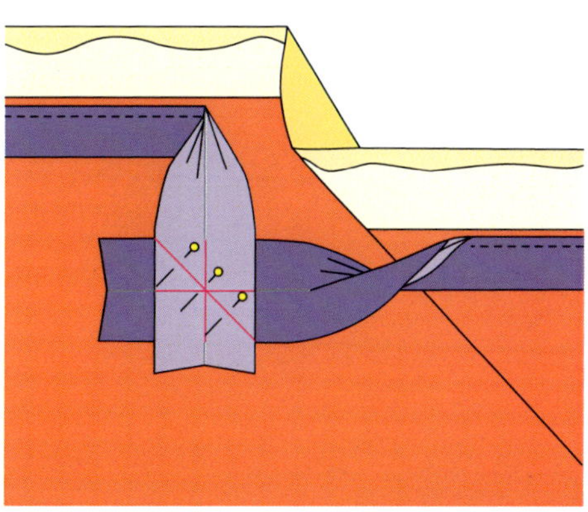

10. Machine stitch along diagonal line **(Fig. 25)**, removing pins as you stitch.

Fig. 25

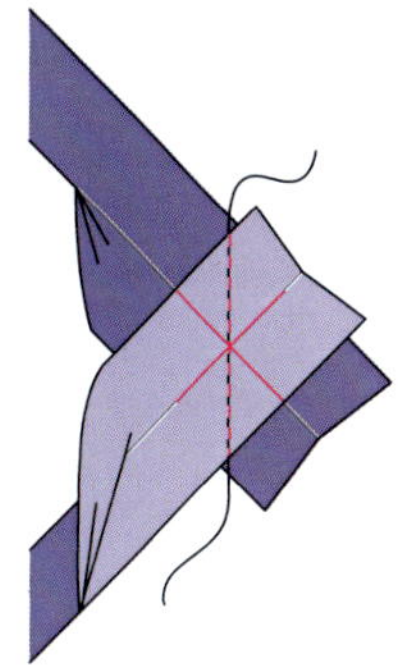

11. Lay binding against quilt to double check that it is correct length.
12. Trim binding ends, leaving $^1/_4$" seam allowance; press seam open. Stitch binding to quilt.
13. If using $2^1/_2$"w binding (finished size $^1/_2$"), trim backing and batting a scant $^1/_4$" larger than quilt top so that batting and backing will fill the binding when it is folded over to quilt backing. If using narrower binding, trim backing and batting even with edges of quilt top.
14. On one edge of quilt, fold binding over to quilt backing and pin pressed edge in place, covering stitching line **(Fig. 26)**. On adjacent side, fold binding over, forming a mitered corner **(Fig. 27)**. Repeat to pin remainder of binding in place.

Fig. 26

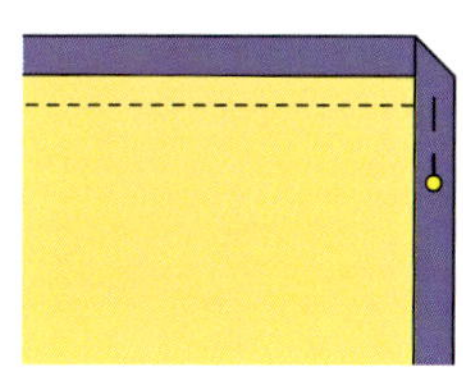

Fig. 27

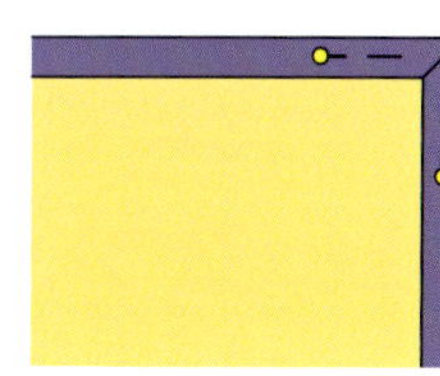

15. Blindstitch binding to backing, taking care not to stitch through to front of quilt.

Fig. 28

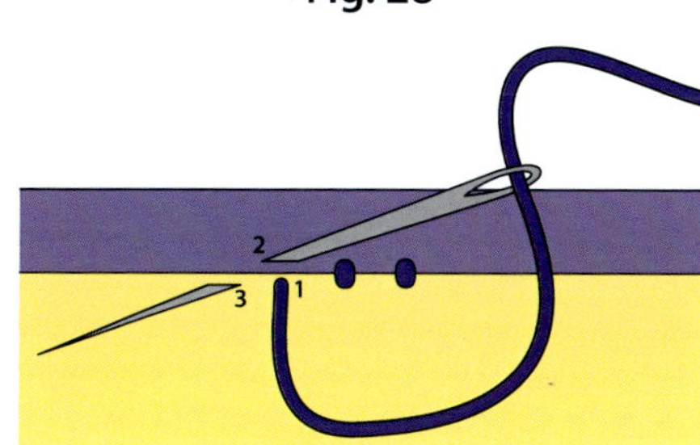

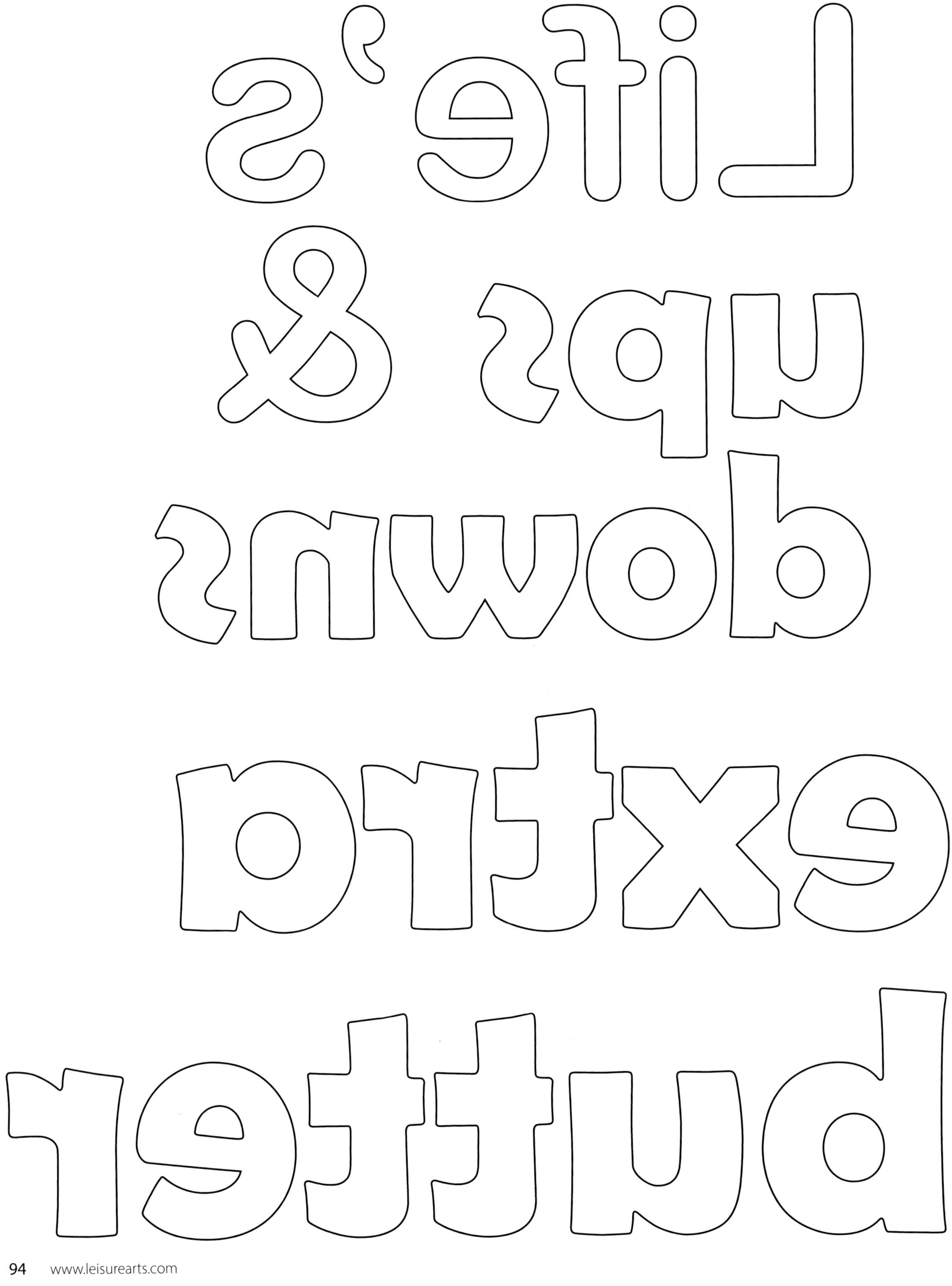
Life's
ups &
downs
extra
butter

Metric Conversion Chart

Inches x 2.54 = centimeters (cm)	Yards x .9144 = meters (m)
Inches x 25.4 = millimeters (mm)	Yards x 91.44 = centimeters (cm)
Inches x .0254 = meters (m)	Centimeters x .3937 = inches (")
	Meters x 1.0936 = yards (yd)

Standard Equivalents

1/8"	3.2 mm	0.32 cm	1/8 yard	11.43 cm	0.11 m
1/4"	6.35 mm	0.635 cm	1/4 yard	22.86 cm	0.23 m
3/8"	9.5 mm	0.95 cm	3/8 yard	34.29 cm	0.34 m
1/2"	12.7 mm	1.27 cm	1/2 yard	45.72 cm	0.46 m
5/8"	15.9 mm	1.59 cm	5/8 yard	57.15 cm	0.57 m
3/4"	19.1 mm	1.91 cm	3/4 yard	68.58 cm	0.69 m
7/8"	22.2 mm	2.22 cm	7/8 yard	80 cm	0.8 m
1 "	25.4 mm	2.54 cm	1 yard	91.44 cm	0.91 m

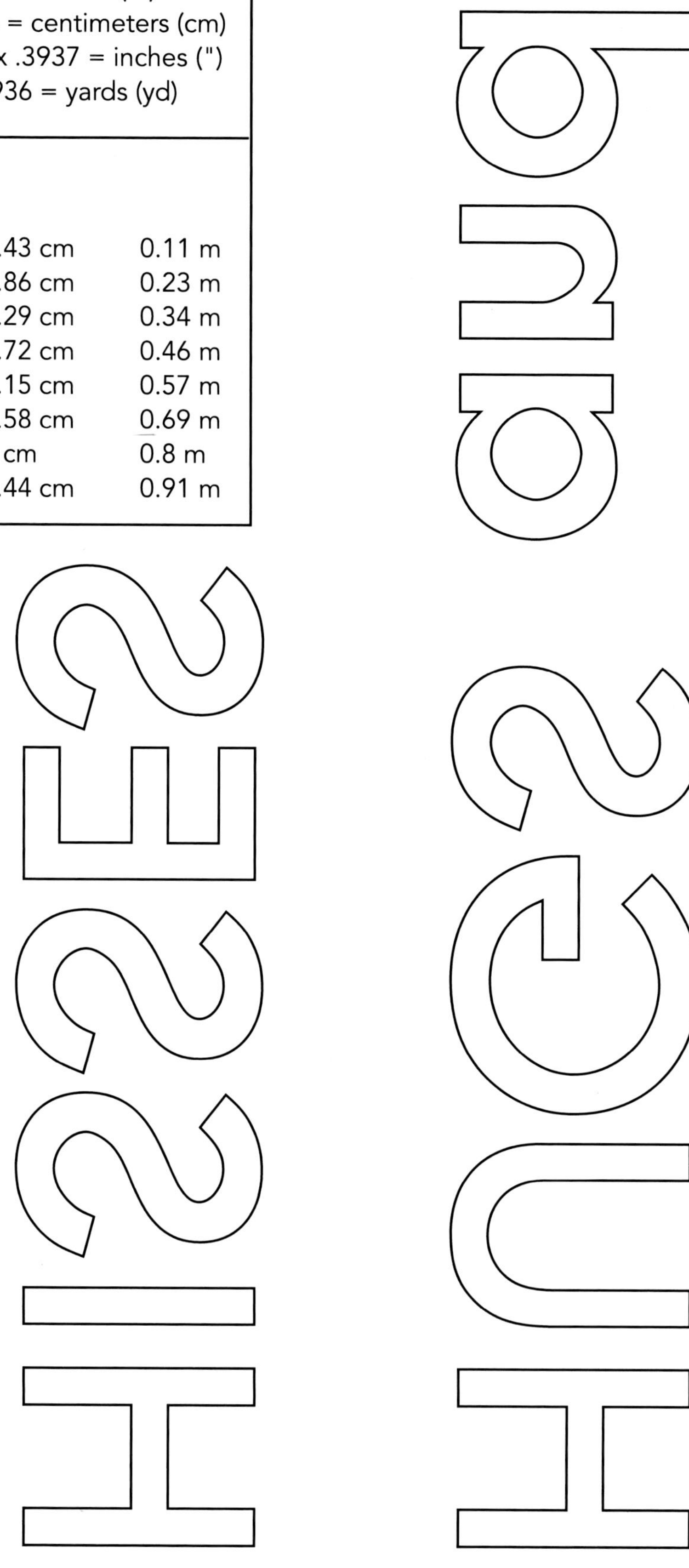

Library of Congress Control Number:
2019952418

Made in U.S.A.

We have made every effort to ensure that these instructions are accurate and complete. We cannot, however, be responsible for human error, typographical mistakes, or variations in individual work.

Technical Editor — Lisa Lancaster
Graphic Designer — Katie Cooper
Photography Stylist — Lori Wenger
Photographer — Jason Masters

Copyright © 2020 by Leisure Arts, Inc., 104 Champs Blvd., STE 100, Maumelle, AR 72113-6738, www.leisurearts.com. All rights reserved.

This publication is protected under federal copyright laws. Reproduction or distribution of this publication or any other Leisure Arts publication, including publications which are out of print, is prohibited unless specifically authorized. This includes, but is not limited to, any form of reproduction or distribution on or through the Internet, including posting, scanning, or e-mail transmission.